...e tribes defeated by Shaka's armies or fleeing from them spread out over ...uth and central Africa. The short lined area indicates Shaka's empire ...atal). Some of the Ndwanduve fled to Lake Victoria (a), some to Nyasaland ..., and some to Mozambique (c). One group of Basutos conquered Barotse- ...nd (d) and another founded a nation in what came to be called Basutoland ... The short broken line indicates the trade routes of the medieval Arabs; ...e long broken line those of the Portuguese.

SHAKA

SHAKA

King of the Zulus

A BIOGRAPHY BY

Daniel Cohen

DOUBLEDAY & COMPANY, INC.

Garden City, New York

1973

CREDITS:

Figures 1 and 2 from *Africa: Her History, Lands, and People* by John A. Williams Copyright © 1962 by Cooper Square Publishers, Inc. Reprinted by permission of Cooper Square Publishers, Inc.
Figure 10 courtesy of *The Illustrated London News*.

ISBN: 0-385-06316-4 Trade
0-385-02509-2 Prebound
Library of Congress Catalog Card Number 73–180066

TO *Naomi Richman*

Contents

An African Conqueror

DURING THE EARLY PART of the nineteenth century, at about the time the empire of Napoleon Bonaparte was breaking up, another great conqueror was just beginning his career on the other side of the equator, in the continent of Africa. His name was Shaka.

Starting with a tiny tribe, Shaka forged his warriors into a formidable military organization. The barefoot Zulu regiments could run fifty miles in a day and fight a pitched battle before the sun went down. Their tight discipline and efficiency matched or surpassed that of the Roman legions with which the Caesars conquered their vast empire.

Shaka changed the nature of warfare in southern Africa, and in so doing completely altered a traditional way of life that had endured for centuries. The explosive force of his conquests scattered the tribes of southern Africa in all directions. Hundreds of miles from the land of the Zulus, tribes of refugees cut swaths of destruction in their efforts to escape the Zulu king.

The very sound of Shaka's name was enough to terrify his enemies and even his own people. If he ordered Zulus to be executed, they would march to their deaths singing his praises. He was the mightiest and most feared conqueror in the known history of black Africa.

Shaka's people sang his praises with chants such as:

> Thou that art great as the sky!
> Thou that art great as the earth!
> Thou that art great as the mountains!
> Thou that art black!
> Thou that art vast as the sea!
> Thou who growest while others are distracted!

It has been estimated that anywhere from one to two million people died as the direct or indirect result of Shaka's wars. Yet while these events were occurring most Europeans, even Europeans in Africa, were completely unaware of them. To Europeans, Africa was still "the dark continent." The interior was a blank spot on their maps. The era of European colonialism had not yet begun.

The Portuguese had been stringing out trading settlements along the African coast since late in the fifteenth century. But the Portuguese settlers were not numerous and did not attempt to venture far inland. Dutch ships had been prowling West African waters since the end of the sixteenth century, and by the middle of the seventeenth century, Dutch settlers had landed at the tip of the African continent. The Dutch were land-hungry and their settlements expanded rapidly, but they had not yet reached the territory of the Zulus by Shaka's time. The British were relative latecomers, particularly in southern Africa. But it was the British who first made contact with Shaka's Zulus.

Not only were most Europeans unaware of Shaka's empire, they could barely conceive that such a thing might exist. Their experience with the black peoples of southern Africa had been limited to contact with small, poor, and generally disorganized tribes.

Stories of Shaka, his army, and his great capital, Bulawayo, "The Place of Killing," gradually filtered into white settlements, but at first they were not believed. So in 1824, when a young English adventurer named Henry Francis Fynn found himself apparently being chased by twenty thousand Zulus, running in perfect formation, he was almost as surprised as he was frightened.

Fynn and other whites were allowed to visit Shaka at "The Place of Killing," and recorded what they saw there. This was how the outside world eventually came to know that in the heart of Africa a black Caesar had mustered his legions and was on the march.

The white observers peppered their journals with exclamations of astonishment at both the pageantry and the brutality of the Zulu court. Shaka himself particularly fascinated these observers, as he has fascinated men ever since. He has been portrayed as a genius and a madman, a hero and a devil incarnate. And the controversy continues.

Shaka's story cannot be lightly dismissed as "ancient history." The results of his brief and bloody career are still being felt in Africa today. From scattered tribes and clans Shaka created a Zulu nation. Though the Zulus are now an oppressed people, they keep alive the tales of the glories of Shaka's age.

SHAKA

I

The Bantu

AROUND THE BEGINNING of the Christian era a black people, the Bantu, began slowly spreading out over a large portion of the African continent. The earliest traces of the Bantu have been found in the Benue River valley near the present border between Nigeria and Cameroon. The Bantu moved south and southeast, through the rain forests of the Congo basin, then fanned out to make new homes in the grasslands of southeastern Africa.

It is not known where the Bantu originally came from, nor can their migrations be traced with any degree of accuracy. The river of migrating people did not move steadily. Some groups stopped and put down roots, others paused and doubled back. But the majority moved on, pushed by the increasing number of new migrants behind them, and pulled by the attraction of new and better land to the south.

The Bantu had no written language. Tales of past wanderings and heroic deeds were passed on from generation to generation by word of mouth. Each clan or family had a specially appointed "praise singer" whose duty it was to recite the formal history of the clan on ceremonial occasions. But the human memory is not very precise, and oral traditions often become confused after a few years. Over the course of centuries they may become hopelessly garbled or be forgotten entirely.

As seminomads, the Bantu were forced to travel light and had few personal possessions. Families lived in huts of wood and leaves, which could be constructed in a matter of hours and destroyed in a matter of minutes. As a result, the Bantu left behind no clear trail of artifacts or ruins by which scientists might trace their progress.

But the Bantu knew how to smelt and work iron, a skill that was unknown to other peoples of southern Africa. Where evidence of ancient iron mining and iron working are found, scientists believe it is a sign that the Bantu once lived in the area.

In the 1770s the Bantu migrating southward literally bumped into white men who were migrating northward. The point of contact was the Great Fish River in what is now the country of South Africa. About a century and a quarter earlier Dutch settlers, who became known as Boers or Afrikaners, first landed at the Cape of Good Hope, the southern tip of Africa. Their settlements spread northward, without much opposition until they met the Xhosa people, southernmost of the Bantu clans, in the valley of the

Great Fish River. Both blacks and whites were surprised by the encounter, for they had almost no knowledge of one another. Previously, the Boers had met only the Bushmen and Hottentots, who could offer little resistance to their advance. The much more numerous blacks, whom the white men called Kaffirs, were a different matter entirely. The Bantu had met other white men, but their only contact was with a few small Portuguese trading colonies on the coast and with bands of shipwrecked sailors. Neither of these experiences led the Bantu to expect the vigorous and deeply entrenched Boers. Nor were the Boers the only whites at the Cape. The Boers were moving north to escape the British, who had begun to dominate the southern tip of Africa.

Today the descendants of the Boers control South Africa. These people say that the Bantu, like themselves, are recent arrivals. This, they claim, gives both Boers and blacks equal title to South Africa. But the evidence of the iron indicates that the Bantu had pushed deeply into southern Africa (though not all the way to the tip of the continent) many centuries before the first Dutch settlers landed there.

When the Bantu began their migrations there was only a small number of them—perhaps just a few hundred. But they prospered, and an exploding population forced them to increase the area under their control. Prior to their coming, central and southern Africa had been thinly populated by other peoples: Pygmies in the rain forests, Bushmen and Hottentots in the drier forests and on the grasslands to the south.

The Pygmies and Bushmen were hunters, while the Hottentots were primarily herders.

The Bantu were a physically larger and stronger people. With their iron-tipped spears they easily overcame any resistance the Pygmies, Bushmen, and Hottentots might have offered. These people were pushed aside and forced to retreat into jungles, deserts, and mountains—sections where the Bantu had no desire to live. If they became troublesome to the Bantu, these more primitive peoples were either absorbed or exterminated.

The word "Bantu" does not describe a nation or a territorial group like the words "American" or "Englishman." It is a linguistic term that comes from a word in the Bantu language that means "people." Sometimes we talk of "English-speaking peoples," referring to Englishmen and Americans as well as Irish, Scots, Canadians, and Australians. The word "Bantu" has a similar meaning.

There is no single Bantu language. Rather, Bantu is a vast collection of related local dialects. Neighboring Bantu groups may speak differing dialects, but they can understand one another quite well. However, the dialects spoken by widely separated Bantu groups might be so different that people could not understand one another at all. Still, the evidence is clear that all of these dialects began with a single language spoken by a single people thousands of years ago.

In less than two thousand years the once-tiny Bantu group populated half a huge continent. Superior weapons and organization allowed them to overcome any opposition. But this cannot explain the explosive

growth of the Bantu population. The area's previous
inhabitants were thinly spread over a great area.
Neither hunting nor simple stock-herding could produce enough food to support a dense population.

The Bantu were both herdsmen and agriculturalists.
They did some hunting, but this was a sideline, a
sport that provided variety to their diet. During the
spring and summer months the Bantu women culti-
vated plots of grain, squash, sweet potatoes, and other
vegetables. These crops, along with milk and milk
products, formed the staples of the ordinary Bantu's
daily diet.

Cattle played an extraordinarily important part in
Bantu life. Men and boys were in charge of the
herds, and in many tribes, women were not even
allowed to enter the cattle pens. Cattle were not only
used for food; in fact, the Bantu did not ordinarily
eat beef because cattle were too valuable to be slaughtered. The animals were slaughtered only for special
feasts or as sacrifices upon the death of a member of
the family, or to appease ancestral spirits.

Milk and milk products, particularly milk curds,
were valued, almost sacred, foods. The Bantu might
generously supply his visitor with vast quantities of
beer, but milk was reserved for family members, or as
a mark of unusual favor. The man who had shared
milk curds with a Bantu family always retained a
special relationship with that family.

Bantu cattle had many other functions as well. The
hides were used for making sandals and shields.
Occasionally cattle were ridden and even raced. Oxen
were often used as pack animals. A few tribes had

specially trained "war cattle" that would charge the enemy lines during a battle. But none of this accounts for the exalted place that cattle occupied in the life of the Bantu. Most significantly, a Bantu's wealth and position in the community—one might say his social status—was determined largely by the number of cattle he possessed. Bantu cattle were small, scraggly, and poorly formed when compared to the highly bred animals found on modern dairy farms or ranches. But they were valued as no prize bull ever has been.

Bantu cattle came in every conceivable color and with every sort of marking. An extraordinarily wealthy man might possess a herd that was all one color, but this was a possession beyond the wildest dreams of the ordinary Bantu.

Hundreds of Bantu words describe the color variation in cattle alone. For identification purposes the ears of cattle were notched, or their horns trained and twisted into fantastic shapes. A good herdsman could describe each individual beast under his care, even if the herd numbered in the hundreds. The Bantu's numbering system was clumsy, and he could not actually count the number of cattle in a big herd, but he was able to recognize each individual animal and so could survey his herd and know almost instantly if a single beast were missing.

Sheep and goats were also raised for milk and meat and to serve as small change in a transaction. Cattle represented the large-denomination bills. They were the Bantu's only luxury and his basic medium of exchange.

The most powerful of Bantu monarchs took as much pride in their herds as they did in their wives or warriors. Even Shaka could sit for hours and watch with contentment as files of his cattle were driven past.

Europeans and Americans have often looked upon the Bantu's attitude toward his cattle as strange and primitive. We might understand this attitude better if we compare it to our own relationship with the automobile. The automobile is, after all, only a means of transportation, and a dangerous and inefficient one at that. Yet many people spend an inordinate amount of money and time on their cars. The Bantu proudly contemplating his cattle is not so very different from the American proudly polishing his new car.

Although herding and agriculture were better means of providing a livelihood for a Bantu family than hunting, the land was not used efficiently. The Bantu knew nothing of irrigation or crop rotation. His fields had a low yield, and the land was quickly exhausted and made useless for planting. Large cattle herds would graze an area into barrenness in a single season. So the Bantu had to find new land on which to grow his crops and graze his cattle, which is why he continually moved on. For centuries there was plenty of new land to move into.

Bantu social structure encouraged expansion. The Bantu were organized into clans or tribes. A clan was a group whose members could trace their descent back to a common ancestor. The tribe was a larger group, containing individuals and families who were not as directly related. The Bantu were polygamous.

A poor man might be able to afford only one wife. A powerful chieftain might have dozens of wives or, in exceptional cases, hundreds of wives. Not all of these wives had the same social position. A chief always had a "great wife," who was usually the daughter of another royal family. Because great wives were expensive—that is, the chief had to pay a considerable dowry or *lobola* in cattle to the bride's family—chiefs often did not marry their great wives until fairly late in life when they were well-established and after they had married several other wives.

The heir to the chief's throne was normally the eldest son of his great wife. But when a chief died he might already have several full-grown sons by minor wives, while his eldest son by his great wife might be only a boy. For this reason the situation at the time of a chief's death was highly unstable. The older sons had often built up a following of their own and so laid claim to the throne. Brothers, uncles, and other male relatives might also claim the throne. The result could be a frantic and bloody scramble for power.

A chief could exercise no real control over families that lived a long distance from him, because each family was a self-sufficient unit. What often happened when disputes arose was that a clan or tribe split and one part moved away. So long as there was plenty of land and the Bantu had no powerful enemies, this system helped to reduce conflict.

The basic social unit of Bantu life was (and is) called the kraal. This word describes both the place where the Bantu family lives and the social group itself. The physical kraal is a circle of beehive-shaped huts, usually surrounded by a hedge or thorny fence. Customarily, the fence had only one opening. At the far end of the kraal opposite the gate stood the largest of the huts. This was the home of the head-man's great wife. The headman would take most of his meals in his great wife's hut but would spend nights where his fancy led him. Other smaller huts around the circle were built for minor wives. The position of a wife's hut in relation to that of the great wife was important in determining the status of that wife and her children. All wives shared their huts with their young children. Grown sons and daughters, other relatives, and family servants might also have huts within the kraal. All of those living within the area made up the social unit called the kraal.

In the center of the circle of huts were the pens in which the cattle were kept. The English word "corral" and the word "kraal" (which is Dutch in origin) have much the same meaning.

The kraals of powerful chiefs were basically the same as those of ordinary men, though they were built on a much larger scale. There was one principal difference: The chief's kraal might have huts for groups of unmarried warriors whose duty it was to serve the chief in battle. Later, chiefs established special military kraals for warriors.

A Bantu child growing up in a kraal had not only to consider his relationship to his own mother and father, but to all of his father's other wives and all their children. These wives were also his "mothers" and their children his "brothers." All his father's brothers were also considered his "father," and often his father's older brothers would play a more important role in his life than his own father. His father's sisters could have an enormous impact on him, too, particularly when he was young.

This complicated network of relationships spread from kraal to kraal. It was far too intricate to work efficiently, and disputes involving cattle, land, and familial obligations often arose between relatives.

In theory, the head of a kraal held absolute power over his wives and children. Disobedience to the headman's command could mean death. In practice, however, wives and older children exercised a considerable degree of independence. The chiefs, who were heads of the royal clan, also theoretically had absolute power over all the other members of the tribe or clan, but they rarely attempted or desired to use such power.

Of the many groups into which the Bantu were divided there was one group whose members all spoke a related variety of dialects called Nguni. These Nguni-speaking peoples lived farther to the south than any of the other Bantu groups. They dwelt primarily in the fertile stretch of land between the Drakensberg Mountains and the coast of the Indian Ocean. The northern boundary of these people was the Powsole River; the southern boundary was the Great Fish River.

The Nguni were not a united group but were fragmented into many small clans and tribes. Among these clans were the Mtetwa and the Zulu.

Recorded Zulu history does not go back very far. Sometime late in the seventeenth century a Nguni chieftain named Mandalela settled his small clan on a patch of land on the White Umfolozi River. When Mandalela died, his son, Zulu, assumed the chieftainship. We know little of Mandalela and almost nothing of Zulu. But whatever Zulu did during his reign, it must have impressed his people, for in generations to follow they took his name for their clan. The word "Zulu" meant "The Heavens," and the clan members styled themselves "The People of the Heavens."

The Zulus were a very small clan. By the end of the eighteenth century, they could not have numbered more than fifteen hundred individuals. Zulu kraals were scattered over an area only about ten miles on each side. The Zulu clan lived completely in the shadow of its larger and more powerful neighbors, particularly the Mtetwa, to whom they were closely related. The story of the Zulu and of Shaka really begins with the Mtetwa and with one of the most enigmatic and attractive figures in all African history —the Mtetwa king Dingiswayo.

II

Dingiswayo

SOMETIME DURING the early years of the nineteenth century (the exact date is not known, but 1808 is the most probable), a strange figure appeared in the Mtetwa royal kraal. The man was without doubt a Mtetwa, but he rode a horse and carried a gun at a time when horses and guns were practically unknown to the Mtetwa. Stranger still, the man claimed to be the rightful king of the Mtetwa. He showed the people a terrible scar on his back as proof of his claim.

Some years earlier the Mtetwa had been ruled by an aging chieftain named Jobe. Jobe's heirs, particularly his oldest son, Tana, became impatient with the old man's longevity. As was common in royal families, Tana decided to speed up his accession to the throne by killing his father, and he enlisted the aid of his younger brother, Godongwana, in the assassination plot. However, Jobe's spies informed him of the plot. One night the old chief sent a band of armed killers to Tana's kraal. Tana was stabbed in his sleep. Godongwana was awakened by the commotion and was able to defend himself. He was seriously wounded by his father's men but managed to fight them off and escape. Godongwana clawed his way through the kraal fence and ran off into the darkness, a barbed assegai or spear sticking out of his back.

Godongwana hid in the bush, where he was secretly tended by one of his sisters. As soon as he was strong enough, he started walking. He knew that he could not stay in or near Mtetwa territory. Jobe's men were searching for him, and it would only be a matter of time until his hiding place was discovered.

Godongwana traveled north, going from clan to clan until he found a place among the Hlubi people, where he felt safe. There he worked as a simple herdsman. He dropped the name Godongwana and took the name Dingiswayo—which has been variously translated as "The Wanderer" or "The Troubled One."

Dingiswayo's activities during his years of exile have been the subject of much controversy. According to one theory he wandered far to the south and lived, for a time, among the white settlers in the Cape of Good Hope Colony. But the Cape Colony was 450 difficult miles from Mtetwa country, and there is simply no reliable evidence that Dingiswayo ever made such a journey. The theory seems to have been the invention of an English governor of the Cape Colony, but it is often reported in modern books.

If Dingiswayo did visit a white settlement, a more reasonable possibility is that he went north to the Portuguese settlement at Delagoa Bay, which was closer. At the time Dingiswayo might have visited it, Delagoa Bay contained only a dozen or so Portuguese officials, traders, and priests and was defended by a ragtag army of castoffs and exiles from surrounding tribes. Few of these soldiers had muskets, and even fewer of the muskets were in working order.

Still, the sight of an army drilling in formation might have awakened in Dingiswayo some ideas about the potential of organized warfare. Later, when Dingiswayo became king of the Mtetwa, he was anxious to open trade relations with the Portuguese at Delagoa Bay, so he obviously knew something about them. But there is no solid evidence that Dingiswayo ever visited Delagoa Bay during his years of wandering.

All traditions concerning Dingiswayo agree, however, that he did meet at least one white man while he was in exile. This man was most probably Robert Cowan, a military surgeon who had been sent overland as an emissary from the British at the Cape Colony to the Portuguese at Delagoa Bay. Dingiswayo may have been employed as a guide for part of the journey, which passed through the region in which he is believed to have been living.

Cowan never reached Delagoa Bay. Sometime during the long and difficult journey he died or was murdered, perhaps by Dingiswayo himself. More

likely, though, Cowan was put to death on the orders
of Chief Pakatwayo of the Qwabe tribe, who believed
the white man to be a *mlungu* or sea monster that
would bring evil upon his tribe. The notion that
white men were sea monsters who lived in huge shells
and fed on the tusks of elephants was widely held
among the Bantu. The belief is not as outrageous as
it first sounds. The sea was an unknown world to
the Bantu. Few of them had ever seen a ship, and
in oral accounts the white men's vessels might easily
have been described as gigantic sea shells. Since white
traders appeared to have an insatiable hunger for
ivory, it might have seemed as though they ate the
elephants' tusks.

At about the time that Dingiswayo was serving as
a guide, he must have heard that his father, Jobe,
had finally died. After Cowan's death, Dingiswayo
took Cowan's horse and gun and returned to his
homeland to claim the throne.

Many historians tend to attribute all of Dingiswayo's later success to his contact with Cowan. But
how much could Dingiswayo have learned from the
English surgeon? At most they spent a few months
together on the trail. Would Cowan have delivered
lectures on European military and civil systems?
Would Dingiswayo have known what he was talking
about if he had? This hardly seems likely. The two
probably had little, if any, knowledge of one another's language, and the interpreters of the time
were notoriously poor.

There is really no reason to claim that it was
some sort of white influence that made Dingiswayo

a great leader. He was a man of tremendous intelligence and skill. Indeed, he might be classed a political genius. More importantly, he rose to power at a time when the old free-and-easy conditions of Bantu life were already breaking down under the pressures of increased population. Once conflicts had been settled by splitting up into small groups and moving to new lands. Now there was no land left into which the new groups could settle, and the reverse process was beginning to take place as larger political units were formed by people who were being squeezed together. Other Bantu chieftains, such as the Ndwandwe under their great chief Zwide, were attempting to do what Dingiswayo ultimately did so very well. The Ngwane of Sobhuze were also bringing large numbers of small clans and tribes under the leadership of a single ruler.

When Dingiswayo arrived back in the country of the Mtetwa, he found that one of his younger brothers, Mawewe, had already taken the throne. Dingiswayo had a stronger claim to the chieftainship, though this did not always mean very much. But Dingiswayo with his rifle and horse and his friends from the days before his exile also had the power to back his claim. Mawewe fled and later was lured back and murdered by Dingiswayo.

It was a bloody, though not unusual, beginning. Dingiswayo had first plotted to kill his father and then driven his brother from the throne, tricked him, and killed him. In later years, however, Dingiswayo was to prove himself to be anything but a bloodthirsty monarch.

While the Mtetwa were more numerous than the Zulus, they were not really a very large group. When he first came to the throne, Dingiswayo might have been able to put five hundred warriors into the field. His entire tribe could not have numbered more than a few thousand. Large armies had been unnecessary in old-style Bantu warfare; indeed, they were impossible to maintain under the fragmented political setup. No single clan or tribe ever grew large enough to have a substantial army.

Before Dingiswayo's time, a mild form of territorial warfare was almost a way of life among the Bantu. The defeated clan might pay a fine of cattle or simply move out of the disputed region. But as less and less land was available, the option of moving away from an enemy was closed off, and the territorial wars became more serious. Larger political units and correspondingly larger armies became an advantage. Dingiswayo soon began to bring defeated clans under his own rule. The result was a loosely structured Mtetwa empire. Surrounding clans were not directly incorporated into the Mtetwa state, but they were made vassals or satellites of the Mtetwa.

According to stories told some years later, Dingiswayo declared that constant fighting among the tribes was against the wishes of God. Therefore, it was his intention to conquer all of the tribes and force them to live in peace with one another. Whether he really had such a grand plan is doubtful, but he did manage to subdue some thirty tribes. His people began calling him The Great One.

Dingiswayo was more successful than other chieftains attempting to establish the same sort of empire because he was more skillful politically. Defeated clans were allowed to retain their land and cattle but had to supply Dingiswayo's army with a specified number of young, unmarried warriors. All able-bodied warriors, married or not, were required to be available for service if Dingiswayo needed them.

Mtetwa rule was not oppressive. If vassal chiefs were loyal to Dingiswayo and remained at peace with their neighbors, they were allowed to rule as their ancestors had, with complete freedom in internal affairs. Particularly independent or troublesome chiefs might be deposed and replaced with more cooperative relatives, but even in such cases Dingiswayo preferred conciliation to confrontation. He repeatedly forgave rebellious chiefs, for he felt that upsetting the traditional authority structure would create more problems than it would solve. Dingiswayo's leniency was both the secret of his success and his ultimate undoing.

Rather than relying on force, Dingiswayo tried to bind together the clans under his control by a complicated series of royal marriages. The result of his efforts was a period of comparative peace among the quarrelsome Nguni clans.

The most conspicuous feature of Dingiswayo's success was the Mtetwa army, which grew enormously and became far more than simply a clan or tribal force. Warriors fought in groups with others of their own age, and promotions were not limited to those who were well born. Any warrior could aspire to a higher position if he showed skill, bravery, and loyalty. Young warriors from many clans were attracted to Dingiswayo's army, since men who held lowly positions in ordinary life had a chance to attain wealth and fame in the service of The Great One.

Among those who came to seek a career in Dingiswayo's army was a young Zulu whose prospects in life had otherwise appeared pretty bleak. He bore the unflattering name of Shaka, "The Parasite."

III

The Outcast

SHAKA WAS AN UNEXPECTED and unwanted child. His father was Senzangakona (The Rightful Doer) a young chieftain of the Zulu clan. His mother was Nandi (The Sweet One), the recently orphaned daughter of a chief of the neighboring Langeni clan. Marriage or any sexual relationship between members of two such closely related clans was forbidden by the complex rules of Nguni kinship, but such taboos were ignored as often as not. Senzangakona and Nandi contrived to meet secretly.

The Nguni-speaking peoples had strict rules regarding sex. These were not so much aimed at the prevention of sexual contact (except between closely related individuals) as at the prevention of pregnancy. Children who were not born to legitimate wives with their own hut in their husband's kraal had no place in the tightly structured Nguni world. There was, however, no moral prohibition concerning sex. This was regarded as a perfectly normal part of life for married and unmarried alike, so long as no pregnancy resulted and the complicated rules of kinship were observed.

One of the Nguni sexual customs is called *uku-hlobonga* (roughly translated this means "the pleasure of the road"). It is a form of incomplete intercourse that serves to release sexual tension but does not result in impregnation. *Uku-hlobonga* was frequently practiced—indeed, encouraged—between young men and unmarried girls. It required a good deal of self-control, but it seemed to work well enough, and few unwanted pregnancies resulted. However, even this activity was forbidden between members of the closely related Zulu and Langeni clans.

A messenger from the Langeni was sent to tell the Zulu elders that Nandi was pregnant and that the father was their chief, Senzangakona. The Langeni asserted that the girl's proper place was now in Senzangakona's kraal as one of his wives.

The Zulu elders were not pleased by this news. Muldi, Senzangakona's half brother, angrily informed the messenger that such a thing was impossible. "Go back home and tell them the girl is only harboring *I-Shaka*," he said. (*I-Shaka* is an intestinal parasite that was commonly believed to cause the symptoms of pregnancy.) Nandi swallowed the Zulu insult and waited.

A few months later another messenger arrived at the Zulu kraals. This time the Zulus were told that

they had better come to pick up Nandi and her
I-Shaka. There could be no denials from the Zulus
now. Muldi's insult stuck, and the infant boy was
named Shaka.

Though they had broken tribal custom, punishment
was out of the question, since Senzangakona was a
chief and Nandi was a chief's daughter. Nandi and
her child were quietly installed in Senzangakona's
kraal. The year was 1787. A short time later they
were married, though the usual ceremonies were
omitted. Nandi's position was that of Senzangakona's
third wife—he had already married his great wife
and another. Ultimately he was to have ten wives.

Nandi entered Senzangakona's kraal under a cloud,
and in the succeeding years the situation did not
improve. As far as Senzangakona was concerned, his
third wife and her child had already caused him
considerable embarrassment and lowered his reputation among his own and neighboring clans.

Nandi was a beautiful, intelligent, and strong-willed
woman. She had expected more from life than to
be the unwanted third wife of the chief of a minor
clan. She had undoubtedly hoped that one of her
own children would become a great chief. Now this
possibility seemed extremely remote. The pair saw
little of one another, although Nandi did bear Senzangakona another child, a girl who was named
Nomcoba.

Nandi's plight was eased somewhat by Senzangakona's great wife, Mkabi. Young wives were customarily entrusted to the care of older wives, and

since Mkabi was related to Nandi's mother, she showed her charge unusual sympathy and kindness.

Bantu children spent the first five years of their lives almost exclusively under the care of their mothers, so the relationship between mother and child was usually close. The relationship between the outcast Nandi and her outcast son became exceptionally close. Nandi was to remain a major influence over Shaka for the rest of his life.

At the age of six, the life of a Bantu boy changed abruptly. He was taken from his mother's protection and sent out to guard the cattle with the other boys of his age group. The work was hard. It began at sunrise and continued until after sundown, no matter what the weather. The job of herdboy was a serious and responsible one. Few allowances were made for youth; none for weakness.

One day, shortly after he had turned six, Shaka was negligent in his duties. He allowed a dog to kill one of his father's sheep. Senzangakona was furious, but Nandi vigorously defended her son. That finished it. The woman had already been enough trouble, and Senzangakona angrily ordered her and her son out of his kraal. It was the privilege of a Zulu husband, particularly a chief, to summarily dismiss his wife in this manner, though it was rarely done.

Nandi and her two children returned to the land of the Langeni, about twenty miles from the Zulu country. Nandi's kinsmen did not receive her warmly. The affair with Senzangakona had disgraced the clan. Besides, they were now forced to return Nandi's *lobola*—the gift of cattle given to a wife's family by her husband. If the marriage was ended by a husband, the gift had to be returned.

Without a husband and with young children to support, Nandi had no real place among the Langeni. She and her children were simply extra mouths to feed. Furthermore, in her years among the Zulus, Nandi had become increasingly headstrong and difficult to deal with. Her presence in the Langeni kraals was thoroughly resented, and much of this resentment spilled over onto Shaka.

To add to his other problems, Shaka's genital organs developed slowly. Since Bantu youths walk about virtually naked until puberty, his undersized genitals were obvious to everyone. This made him the object of every cruel joke the other herdboys could devise. Shaka was never allowed to forget the unfortunate circumstances of his birth nor his own slow physical development. Small wonder the boy grew up lonely, brooding, and embittered. He grew to hate the Langeni clan with particular vehemence.

Shaka's only solace was his mother, who tried her best to protect him from the hostile outside world. According to Zulu legends, Nandi used to console her son by telling him that one day he would be the greatest chief in the land. "I can see it in your eyes. When you are angry they shine like the sun, and yet no eyes can be more tender when you speak comforting words to me in my misery."

During these unhappy years, Shaka and his mother continued to be befriended by Senzangakona's great wife Mkabi and by Langanzana, Senzangakona's fourth wife, and several others. Shaka was to remember the few friends of his youth, he was also to remember his enemies.

When Shaka was in his teens—around the year 1802—a terrible famine struck the land of the Langeni. It was called the famine of Madlatule ("eat what you can and say nothing").

Even in good times Nandi and her children had been only tolerated by the clan. During the famine there was no food to spare for them, and they were once again forced to wander. The family lived for a time among the Qwabe tribe under the protection of a man named Gendyana. Here the facts become a little unclear. It appears that Nandi had already borne Gendyana a son. No matter how little Senzangakona cared for Nandi, he might well have considered this an open case of adultery and demanded death for both Nandi and Gendyana. But neither Senzangakona nor anyone else seems to have bothered much about the incident.

By this time Shaka had passed puberty and had not only begun to develop normally but had acquired a magnificent physique. He had also displayed exceptional bravery, skill, and quick intelligence on several occasions. Shaka's relatives began to look at him with new eyes. Previously he had been just an ordinary herdboy, but soon he would be old enough to become a warrior, a welcome and valued addition to any clan. Both the Zulus and the Langeni began to press Nandi for the return of her son.

Senzangakona may have been more anxious to eliminate Shaka as a potential threat to the Zulu throne then to employ him as a warrior. According to one tradition—a doubtful one, admittedly—Senzangakona planned to have Shaka killed, but the chief who was to arrange the murder refused to do so and warned Shaka of the plan. When Shaka had returned briefly to the land of the Zulus for his puberty ceremony, which was traditionally held in the father's kraal, he behaved coldly and arrogantly toward Senzangakona. This touched off another quarrel, and the two parted in great anger.

In about 1803 Nandi decided to find a more powerful protector for herself and her children. They went to the kraal of Nandi's father's sister, who was a member of the Deletsheni clan, a subdivision of the powerful Mtetwa tribe. There Nandi and her children lived under the protection of a man called Mbiya, whom Shaka came to regard as his foster father. The following years were comparatively happy ones for the outcasts.

These same years were momentous for the Mtetwa. It was during this period that the aging king Jobe discovered the assassination plot of his two sons Tana and Godongwana. It was also the period when the fugitive Godongwana, now calling himself Dingiswayo, returned with his horse and gun to claim the Mtetwa throne.

Shaka had grown to a height of over six feet, half a head taller than the average Bantu. His huge frame was heavily muscled. Senzangakona and many of his sons grew quite fat, but Shaka never allowed himself to overeat and engaged in vigorous physical activity. He also became an expert in the use of the light throwing assegai, the principal Nguni weapon of war.

Though Shaka hated his father, he was intensely
conscious of his own royal blood and looked down
upon all those less well born. Despite this, he was
admired by the others of his age group for his strength
and bravery. They looked up to him as a natural
leader.

The young men of Shaka's age were potential re-
cruits for Dingiswayo's army. All those from one
region or clan and one age group were organized into
a group called a *Ntagna*. They were then sent to live
in special military kraals maintained by a chief and
were called upon to fight in the chief's wars. Each
Ntagna was commanded by its own leader, and Shaka
was made the leader of his group. When he was
twenty-three years old, Shaka's entire group was
called to serve in Dingiswayo's *Izi-cwe* regiment.
Shaka remained a part of the Mtetwa army for six
years, and his fortunes rose along with those of
Dingiswayo.

Dingiswayo was not primarily a warrior, but in
order to fulfill his plan of placing most of the Nguni
chiefs under his overlordship, he was forced to organize his army more effectively than his neighbors did.
Dingiswayo employed regiments based on age rather
than the traditional tribal groups but made no major
military innovations. He was content to let his
warriors fight along mostly traditional lines, which
meant that they were not a very efficient force.

Before population pressure drove the clans and
tribes into fierce competition for agricultural and graz-
ing land, warfare had been more of a sport than a
serious contest. The typical warrior was armed with a

handful of light, steel-tipped throwing assegais. His only protection was an oxhide shield, which might be as tall as the warrior himself. Bows and arrows were never used, although the Bantu knew about them. There was no wood in the region suitable for making a strong and flexible bow. The Bushmen had used the bow and arrow for hunting, but their bows were weak, and the arrows had little force. They had to rely on poison-tipped arrows to bring down their prey.

Bantu armies fought in a mob called an *impi*. There was little internal organization or leadership; in general each warrior fought as an individual. Individual bravery rather than strategy or tactics was the key to victory.

Two armies would approach one another shouting war cries, insults, and threats. When they got within throwing distance, or about fifty yards, the warriors would hurl their assegais. The spears did little damage, for they were usually blocked by the shields of the opposing army. A well-thrown assegai could penetrate an oxhide shield at fifty yards, but assegais were rarely thrown accurately, since the warriors crowded so closely together that they did not have sufficient throwing room.

Most of the damage in a battle was done at close quarters. Each warrior would retain one assegai to use as a stabbing weapon. He might also carry a knobkerry, a stick with a knob on the end that was used for bashing skulls. When their throwing spears were exhausted, the two armies would clash in hand-to-hand combat until one side or the other threw down their shields and ran away. With that the battle was over.

A warrior who had killed another in battle had to undergo elaborate purification ceremonies before he could once again join the normal life of the tribe. Shipwrecked sailors who had wandered among the Nguni-speaking Bantu as early as the seventeenth century commented that at the time the Nguni seemed to have a particularly high regard for human life. The sailors noted that they could say nothing of the courage of the people, for they had never observed any wars.

There were few casualties in a traditional battle. Occasionally, Nguni warfare would assume an even more ritualized character. As the *impis* approached one another, shouting threats, a leading warrior from one side would rush forward and challenge the strongest warrior from the opposing army to engage in single combat. In this case the winner of the fight determined the outcome of the entire battle. Medieval European knights also employed the ritual of using champions in single combat to determine the outcome of a battle.

The chief did not customarily lead his army into battle, nor did he expose himself to danger. Instead he might sit on a nearby hill, accompanied by some of his wives and children to watch. Often great crowds of women and children would also gather to watch and would cheer their side. There was no danger, even if their side lost, that the victors would sweep down and kill or capture them.

If any warriors were captured in battle they were

quickly ransomed with cattle. The losing side might pay a fine in cattle or might move out of the disputed region, but there were no more serious consequences. A battle that began at noon would be over by evening. Since most battles were fought with immediate neighbors, warriors often did not have to spend so much as a single night away from their home kraals. Long marches or extended campaigns were unknown.

Under Dingiswayo and other Nguni chiefs of the early nineteenth century, warfare became much more than a spectator sport. The price of losing a battle was no longer just a few cattle or a short move. Defeated clans were forced to become vassals of Dingiswayo's empire. Though Dingiswayo proved to be a lenient master, many clans resented the loss of complete independence. Battles, particularly those between Dingiswayo's Mtetwa army and the army of Zwide's Ndwande confederation, were longer and bloodier than anything the Nguni had known before. Dingiswayo's armies often took savage retribution against clans that rebelled or resisted, but after the clans submitted, their resistance would be forgiven. The Nguni peoples had not yet entered the era of total warfare.

Shaka fit well into the role of warrior. As a member of the *Izi-cwe* regiment he fought Dingiswayo's enemies with all the strength and courage at his command. Dingiswayo recognized the young Zulu's value, and Shaka rose to become commander of the *Izi-cwe* regiment.

Though he never ventured to oppose Dingiswayo,

Shaka regarded the Mtetwa methods of warfare as
old-fashioned and even foolish. The light throwing
assegai, Shaka reasoned, was ill-suited to the demands of serious warfare. Shaka designed a short
stabbing assegai to replace the throwing weapons. The
new assegai had a broad blade and a heavy, short-
ened shaft. It was to be used in close combat and
wielded with an underhand thrust. Though it resembled a spear, Shaka's new assegai was actually
used like a sword. It was, in fact, remarkably similar
to the famous short sword with which the legions of
ancient Rome conquered their empire.

According to Zulu legend, when Shaka decided to
have a stabbing assegai made for himself, he went
to see the most celebrated blacksmith in the region, a
man named Ngonyama (The Lion). Among the
Bantu, a blacksmith was considered half craftsman,
half wizard. Traditionally, blacksmiths surrounded
their trade with a great deal of mysterious ritual.
Since one of the necessary elements for making good
iron was reputed to be human fat, ordinary people
avoided the kraals of the blacksmiths whenever possible, fearing that they might wind up as part of the
smelting process. This aura of fear helped the blacksmiths preserve their trade secrets.

But Shaka went boldly to Ngonyama's kraal and
told him what he needed. Usually the celebrated
blacksmith charged very dearly for his work, and
Shaka, being poor, could not have paid much. However, in this case Ngonyama asked for only a single
cow, and even that payment was postponed until

some future time. The blacksmith was said to have recognized Shaka's greatness.

The new broad blade was prepared with all the care necessary and with all the ceremonies that were supposed to endow it with magical properties. The finished product was more than a weapon; it was almost a magical object. Medieval knights had much the same attitude toward their swords and for the same reasons. Good metal weapons that would not shatter or crack under the blows of a battle were expensive and hard to come by. The knights often named their swords. Shaka, too, had a name for his weapon; he called it *Ixwa*. In the Zulu language the "X" is pronounced with a tongue click, somewhat like the noise made by a driver urging on his horse. Many believe that Shaka named his weapon *Ixwa* to imitate the sound of an assegai being pulled out of a wound after a deep thrust. The blade itself was slightly wavy and clung to the flesh so that when withdrawn, it made a sucking noise.

In order to use the stabbing assegai effectively, the shield also had to be wielded as an offensive weapon. The shield was carried on the left arm. When in close quarters with an opponent, Shaka would hook the left edge of his shield over the left edge of his opponent's shield. With a powerful backhand sweep he could pull his opponent nearly off balance. This maneuver accomplished two things. First, it kept Shaka's left side covered by his own and his adversary's shield, so that he was not open to a thrust from the other's assegai, which was pointed at him from that side. At the same time it exposed the

enemy warrior's left side to Shaka's thrust. The outcome of such an encounter was swift. Shaka's weapon
would plunge straight to the heart, and the victim
would be pulled off the blade by the weight of his
own falling body. As the enemy crumpled to the
ground, Shaka would shout *"Ngadla!* [I have eaten!]."

Other military innovations followed, the most con-
troversial of which was Shaka's decision to abandon
the oxhide sandals that warriors traditionally wore
in favor of fighting barefoot. The sandals protected the
feet well enough, but they were cumbersome. They
slowed a man down and made his footing unsure on
rough and rocky ground. But the country was dotted
with thorny plants and sharp rocks, and a warrior's
soles had to be heavily calloused in order for him to be
able to run barefoot without cutting his feet badly.
Since hardening the feet was a long and painful process, at first only a few of Shaka's most devoted associates in the *Izi-cwe* regiment joined him in fighting
without sandals.

When Dingiswayo ordered his army against Chief
Pungashe of the Butelezi, Shaka had his first opportunity to show what the new methods of battle could
accomplish. Ironically, the Butelezi were neighbors
of the Zulu and had forced the Zulus into an
alliance, so Shaka was fighting against many of his
own people. Shaka's half brother Bakuza, one of
Senzangakona's favorite sons, was in the ranks of the
enemy army.

The Butelezi was badly outnumbered by Dingiswayo's troops, but they rejected The Great One's
offer of leniency and tried to make a stand. One of

the Butelezi's best warriors stepped forward and challenged a member of the advancing *Izi-cwe* regiment to single combat. Shaka enthusiastically accepted the challenge, but he did not intend to fight according to the old rules. Instead of standing fifty yards from the Butelezi warrior and exchanging throwing spears, he brushed aside the spears thrown by his opponent and rushed straight toward him. With a single unbroken motion, Shaka swept the Butelezi's shield to the side and stabbed him under the left armpit. The *Izi-cwe* were almost as astonished as the enemy at the swift outcome of the contest. Nor did Shaka stop there. All alone, he charged the entire Butelezi force. After a second's hesitation his close companions and then the entire *Izi-cwe* regiment followed him.

The Butelezi, accustomed to the old ways of fighting, dropped their shields and fled in panic, but Shaka would not recognize this traditional sign of surrender. His warriors pursued the fleeing Butelezi so ferociously that Dingiswayo himself finally had to call a halt to the slaughter. The casualties incurred during the encounter were extremely high. Fifty Butelezi warriors were killed and about twenty of Dingiswayo's men. Among those killed was Shaka's half brother Bakuza. The stunned Pungashe quickly accepted Dingiswayo's overlordship.

More significantly (though it did not seem so at the time), the battle convinced Senzangakona, chief of the Zulus, to become a vassal of Dingiswayo. The Zulus had been regularly defeated by the Butelezi, and Senzangakona knew that he could not hope to stand against those who had so easily defeated his conquerors.

The battle also brought Shaka to the direct attention of Dingiswayo, who appreciated and respected Shaka's fighting abilities and also saw in him a future political ally. For the time being Dingiswayo was content to allow Senzangakona to rule his own people as he had in the past. But if Senzangakona should die, or become troublesomely independent, then Shaka, a member of the Zulu royal family, might be installed as chief. Dingiswayo believed that Shaka was a man to be trusted; it was by such calculations that The Great One had patched together his empire.

Shaka was rewarded for his success in battle by being given increased responsibility within the Mtetwa army. He was also given a herd of cattle. For the first time in his life, he was no longer a poor man.

In subsequent battles the *Izi-cwe* regiment, under Shaka's energetic command, continued to distinguish itself, and Shaka began to experiment with what was to become the famous and feared Zulu "head, horns, and chest formation." Rather than just charging in a mass, his warriors were divided into groups. In the center of the line was the "head"—several files of men who faced the enemy directly. Fanning out on both sides of the "head" were the curved "horns." These two groups tried to outflank and encircle the enemy. Behind the "head" was the "chest." This was a large body of warriors kept in reserve. They were not to fight or even to show themselves until the appropriate moment. Thus the enemy might be deceived as to the numbers it faced. The "head, horns, and chest formation" may have been entirely Shaka's invention, but more likely it was an adaptation of the Bantu hunt, in which game would be encircled and everything trapped within the circle slaughtered.

Rather than continually shouting taunts at the enemy, Shaka's warriors maneuvered in silence, so that they could hear the commands of their officers and react swiftly. Most important of all, discipline and mass action took the place of the single hero. Warriors were ordered not to rush forward on their own under any circumstances. To drive home the lesson, Shaka sometimes told his reserve unit to sit with their backs to the battle so that they could not see what was going on. This prevented warriors from getting carried away and rushing in prematurely.

Shaka's troops were drilled relentlessly in the use of the stabbing assegai and the shield. Shaka also organized the older herdboys, those fifteen or sixteen years of age and as yet below the age of full warrior, as the *dubi,* the keepers of supplies. One of these boys was assigned to every three warriors. His job was to carry supplies, extra weapons, and when needed, water.

Though he was a harsh and demanding commander, Shaka could also be a generous one. He gave more than the usual share of captured cattle to his men, keeping little or nothing for himself.

Shaka's influence spread throughout Dingiswayo's army. Eventually he joined the other important personages or *indunas* in the king's councils.

In theory, a Bantu chief was all-powerful. In fact, he was compelled to accept the advice of the important elders of the community and of others such as the military *indunas*. The elders were usually profoundly conservative and acted as the keepers of tradition. A king who flouted tradition too openly might find himself removed by rebellion or assassination. Or his tribe might break up, his subjects moving away to join rivals. Even as powerful a monarch as Dingiswayo could not ignore the elders. Just as the power of the monarch was limited, so was the influence of younger members of the tribe. Shaka was much admired on the battlefield, but in the councils he had to speak quietly and moderately.

It is difficult to assess Shaka's attitude toward Dingiswayo. Certainly he felt that Dingiswayo's policy of leniency toward defeated clans and tribes was pointless. As a warrior, he knew that he often had to defeat the same enemy on two or three different occasions. After each defeat the enemy was allowed to retain most of his cattle and lands. A defeated chief would merely bide his time until he felt strong enough to rebel once again. Shaka advised a policy of *impi ebomvu* (red impi)—which meant total war against army and civilian population alike. His reasoning was, "Strike an enemy once and for all. Let him cease to exist as a tribe or he will live to fly at your throat again." Shaka was particularly anxious to see that Zwide of the Ndwandwe, Dingiswayo's most powerful and resourceful enemy, be wiped out. Shaka's plan was supported by many of the other military commanders, but Dingiswayo and the older *indunas* favored a continued policy of moderation and conciliation.

Dingiswayo was thoroughly convinced of Shaka's loyalty and attempted to make certain that Shaka would become the Zulu chief. Senzangakona was growing old and had become tremendously fat. His health was poor, and his grown sons were already intriguing for the throne. Senzangakona was called to Dingiswayo's kraal and brought face to face with the son he had once rejected and had not seen for ten years. Dingiswayo pointed out that Shaka would make an excellent heir to the Zulu throne and that he himself strongly favored the idea. Senzangakona professed to be delighted with the suggestion, and perhaps he really was. At the time Shaka was Senzangakona's oldest surviving son, and so had a good claim to the throne. In addition, Shaka had proved himself to be a great warrior and a natural leader. Most important of all, he was Dingiswayo's favorite.

But after Senzangakona returned home, he changed his mind about the succession and decided in favor of Sigujana, a son of his eighth wife. Senzangakona died early in the year 1816. The news of his death was not made public for several days, and Sigujana used the time to consolidate his hold on the throne and to eliminate all the potential rivals that he could reach. By the time word of Senzangakona's death reached Shaka, Sigujana had successfully claimed Zulu leadership.

Shaka was furious at this turn of events. He promptly sent his younger half brother, Ngwadi, son

of Nandi by her liaison with Gendyana, to see Sigujana. Ngwadi was instructed to tell the new Zulu
chief to abdicate or suffer the consequences. Instead,
Ngwadi gained Sigujana's confidence and then killed
him. Whether this was part of a prearranged plan,
or whether Ngwadi simply lost his temper when confronted with Sigujana's refusal to step aside, is unknown. Either alternative is possible. Shaka was
certainly not above treachery, but Ngwadi was fanati-
cally devoted to his half brother and could easily have
taken matters into his own hands.

In any case Shaka, once a despised and homeless
exile, now assumed the chieftaincy of the Zulu clan.

IV

The King

In 1816 Shaka entered his father's kraal, where he had spent so many unhappy years. This time he came as chief of the Zulus, marching at the head of the *Izi-cwe* regiment. As an independent chief in his own right, Shaka could no longer be commander of the regiment, which was still a part of Dingiswayo's Mtetwa army, but Dingiswayo had sent the soldiers along to make sure that the transfer of the Zulu chieftainship to his protégé went smoothly.

The occasion seemed as much a triumph for Dingiswayo as for Shaka himself. According to the Zulu chronicles, Ngomane, the new commander of the *Izi-cwe* regiment, assembled the Zulu headmen and told them:

"Children of Zulu! Today I present to you Shaka, son of Senzangakona, son of Jama, descended from

Zulu, as your lawful chief. So says The Great One [Dingiswayo], whose mouth I am. Is there anyone here who can contest the righteousness of this decision? If so, let him stand forth and speak now, or hereafter be silent."

There must have been dissatisfaction. Shaka had several other half brothers who had some claim to the throne. But the meaning behind the presence of Dingiswayo's *Izi-cwe* regiment was not lost on the Zulus, and they remained silent.

If the Zulus believed that their new king was a mere puppet of the Mtetwa chief, Shaka soon disabused them. From the very first his aim was to completely change Zulu society and to create a fighting machine, against which no power in Africa could stand. And he intended to make these changes quickly.

Anyone who failed to show sufficient enthusiasm for the new chief was immediately eliminated. The first to be executed was Shaka's uncle Muldi, who had sent the insulting *I-Shaka* message when he first learned of Nandi's pregnancy. Muldi, say the Zulu legends, went to his death bravely, and his last words were a prediction of Shaka's future greatness.

Shaka's most pressing order of business was to create an army, for up to that time no Zulu army had existed. All Zulu males who were capable of fighting were called before the new chief.

Among the Zulus different ages or stations in life were marked by symbols or costumes. Men who were married or were of marriageable age wore a headring, a circle of fibrous fungus material that was sewn into the hair, plastered with beeswax, and polished to a high shine. Shaka organized the married men between the ages of thirty and forty into the *Ama-Wombe* regiment. These men were allowed to retain their wives and social position, but they were forced to spend much of their time living in a newly established military kraal.

The unmarried men who wore the headring were forced to shave it off (indicating that they were no longer eligible for marriage) and to join the other unmarried men in the *Izim-Pohlo* or "Bachelors Brigade."

Shaka's greatest hope lay in the new *I-Fasimba* regiment. This was made up of the oldest of the herdboys, youths of about twenty. The older men had had some experience in battle, but they had learned to fight by the traditional methods, which Shaka intended to discard. Further, these warriors had no particular pride, since Zulu military history up to that time had been largely a series of humiliating defeats. The young men, fresh from the difficult but toughening job of tending herds, knew little of past tactics or of past defeats. These were the men Shaka intended to mold into a tireless and invincible fighting machine. Soon this regiment came to be called "Shaka's Own."

Probably not more than four hundred men of military age were available to answer the first summons of the new Zulu chief. The "Bachelors Brigade" had to be divided into two groups so that Shaka could have four regiments for the "head, horns, and chest" of his favorite military formation.

Within a month after he assumed leadership, Shaka began building his new royal kraal. The name he chose for his home was to give a very clear indication of his future policy. He called it Bulawayo—"The Place of Killing."

While workers were building the royal kraal, all available blacksmiths were engaged in turning out broad-bladed stabbing assegais to replace the old throwing weapons. Shaka also ordered the making of larger and stronger shields, more suitable for the sort of warfare he intended to pursue.

The regiments were drilled mercilessly in the use of their new weapons and in battlefield maneuvers. The unfamiliar weapons were adopted easily enough, but when Shaka ordered the Zulu warriors to throw away their sandals and train in bare feet, there was much grumbling. A month after he had given the command to discard the sandals, it had not yet been fully obeyed.

As a result, Shaka devised a demonstration of the penalty for disobedience. He had his men collect quantities of a plant called the devil thorn, which has long, sharp spikes. The prevalence of this plant was one of the reasons why the Zulu warriors objected to going without their sandals. The devil thorns were scattered around the central cattle enclosure of Bulawayo, which commonly served as a parade ground and general meeting place.

Summoning his troops, Shaka told them he had heard of the dissatisfaction that had accompanied his order to discard their sandals. He said that as a means of helping the men harden their feet he had had the parade ground covered with thorns, which the warriors were to stamp into the earth with their bare feet. Anyone who hesitated, or who did not seem to be stamping with sufficient zeal, was to be considered disobedient to the king's command. "And disobedience merits death. My slayers are at hand."

Shaka led the regiments into the parade ground and demonstrated how the stamping should be done. Since he had not worn sandals in many years, his feet were as tough as oxhide, and he was able to stamp down the sharp thorns with ease. Chanting a war song, the Zulu army tried to imitate their leader. Shaka pointed out those men who seemed to be holding back. They were immediately clubbed to death by the slayers, professional killers who traditionally served the chief. After about a half dozen were killed, the rest of the Zulu army went into a frenzy of stamping. When Shaka was satisfied with the performance, he ordered a generous measure of beer and beef for his men.

Thus the pattern of Zulu discipline was laid down. Ample rewards for those who obeyed; immediate death for those who did not. Shaka had begun to establish himself as the great provider-destroyer.

Still, Shaka's army remained tiny, and the area in which the Zulus could operate was extremely limited. They were under the shadow of the Mtetwas and could not afford to attack or even annoy Dingiswayo or any of Dingiswayo's other vassals. However, Zulu territory was on the fringe of the Mtetwa sphere of influence. Shaka knew that Dingiswayo would not be upset if he built Zulu power at the expense of outlying clans. Indeed, it was because Dingiswayo had wanted a Zulu buffer state between his own territory and that of other large and powerful aggregations that

he had so actively supported Shaka in the first place.
As long as Shaka moved with caution and did not give
Dingiswayo the idea that he was building a rival state,
he could count on the continued backing of The
Great One.

The first to feel the new Zulu might were the
Langeni, Nandi's people, the clan that had treated
both Nandi and Shaka so badly. One morning the
Langeni awoke to find their main kraal surrounded
by the Zulu *impis*. No resistance was offered; none
was possible, for the Langeni, like the Zulus before
Shaka, had no real army.

In the years since he had dwelt among the Langeni,
Shaka had neither forgotten nor forgiven the slights
that he and his mother had suffered. He had practically the entire clan brought before him. All those
who had tormented him or been unkind to his mother
were divided into two groups, according to the serious-
ness of their offense. Among the accused, any who
could recall a single act of kindness toward the Zulu
chief and his mother were asked to speak. One man
said that he had once brought Nandi a special grind-
ing stone. It was a small favor, but Shaka remem-
bered it. The favor was acknowledged, and Shaka
pardoned the man, though he had been insulted by
him many times. All the rest were to pay their debt to
Shaka by "eating earth"—being killed.

Those who had been guilty of relatively minor insults were to be clubbed to death. The rest were to
suffer the agonizing death of impalement on sharp
wooden stakes. Their bodies were to be left exposed
as an example of the fate that awaited all those who

dared insult Shaka. According to Zulu legend, those who were to suffer the easier death were grateful and marched off to their execution with the exclamation *"Baba nkosi!* [Father and chief!]"

Many have concluded that even early in his career, Shaka was a monster who enjoyed the painful death of his enemies. But it is quite clear that while Shaka had no particular sympathy for human suffering, he did not relish it either. There is considerable testimony that Shaka himself rarely observed the most brutal of the executions he ordered and that he would only watch those carried out by the relatively humane methods of neck breaking or stabbing.

Shaka's success against the Langeni frightened several other small clans in the vicinity into forming alliances with the Zulus. The principal result of these alliances was that many more young men were attracted to Shaka's army. Despite the tight discipline, hardship, and danger, the service did offer young men a chance for advancement, which was denied them in ordinary life.

When the Zulu army reached about twice its original size, Shaka decided to move against a more formidable foe. He chose the Butelezi tribe, which lived to the west of the Zulus. The Butelezi and the Zulus were old enemies. In past wars the Zulus had almost invariably been defeated. Shaka's father had been captured by the Butelezi several times, and Shaka's half brothers had been forced to serve in the Butelezi army.

Pungashe, the chief of the Butelezi, was unaware that conditions in the land of the Zulus had changed

under Shaka's leadership. Though he had been badly
defeated by Dingiswayo, Pungashe had rebelled at the
first opportunity. Shaka himself had led the army
that crushed the Butelezi, but Pungashe had no respect for him. He contemptuously referred to Shaka as
"Dingiswayo's poor man." Shaka heard of this and
sent an emissary to Pungashe demanding an apology.
He received in answer another expression of contempt.
Shaka used this as a pretext to declare war.

Pungashe had learned nothing from his initial defeat by Shaka. The Butelezi chief expected another
old-fashioned war, and thought his larger army would
insure victory. In fact, the Zulu army now outnumbered that of the Butelezi. Shaka saw no reason to in-
form his opponent of this change in relative strength
until it was too late for the Butelezi to do anything
about it. He therefore ordered his men to stand close
together, their shields to their sides, so that from a distance they would look like a smaller force. Approximately 750 Zulus were sent to oppose 600 Butelezi.

Chief Pungashe sat on a hilltop overlooking the
battlefield. As usual, he was accompanied by the
tribal elders and many of the Butelezi women and
children. Shaka, on the other hand, stood in the midst
of his own men, and since he was half a head taller
than any of them, he could see clearly everything that
was going on. From this position he was able to direct
the battle and personally observe any warriors who
were disobedient or cowardly.

The two armies advanced to within about sixty
yards of one another. On an order from Shaka, the
"horns" of the Zulu battle formation quickly spread

out to begin their encircling movement. The surprised Butelezi let fly a shower of spears, which did almost no damage. The Zulu army had been quiet to this point, but now they shouted their war cry *"Sigidi!* [The strength of a thousand!]," and the "head" of the Zulu formation crashed straight into the Butelezi ranks.

The Zulu warriors used their stabbing assegais with deadly efficiency. Few among them missed the chance to proclaim *"Ngadla!"* after a kill. The Butelezi tried to escape, but there was no place they could go, for they had been surrounded by the swift-running Zulu "horns." Warriors who threw down their shields in the traditional sign of surrender were slain along with whose who continued fighting. Every Butelezi on the field, including the women spectators, fell beneath the Zulu assegais. Chief Pungashe and a handful of attendants were the only ones who were able to escape the slaughter.

The battle itself was over in less than an hour. Then the Zulus fanned out over the battlefield, killing the Butelezi wounded. The dead men's stomachs were slit open to "allow their spirits to escape." This mutilation of the dead has often been looked upon as an act of sheer savagery, but it had a practical effect. Bodies that had been opened tended to dry out, rather than to become bloated and rotten, as they otherwise would have under the blazing African sun. A battlefield full of rotting corpses was a place where disease could start.

Wounded Zulus were carefully tended by their companions. Those whose wounds were grave and who appeared beyond help were asked if they wished to be put out of their misery. Invariably they said "Yes." For those who were unconscious or otherwise beyond answering, agreement was assumed. Shaka saw no point in letting a badly wounded man, who was going to die anyway, linger on in agony. A quick thrust of the assegai was kinder.

The Zulus then ranged through the Butelezi kraals, capturing the women and children and rounding up the cattle. Those of both sexes who seemed old or useless were killed at once. Finally, the Butelezi huts were burned to the ground.

This was the *impi ebomvu*—the total war—that Shaka had often preached in the councils of Dingiswayo. Shaka was well pleased with the results of the day. His army had utterly destroyed one of the Zulus' oldest enemies. His own losses had been surprisingly light, and his stock of cattle was considerably increased. Now, for the first time, Shaka's name began to inspire fear, or at least apprehension in the kraals of the great chiefs of southern Africa.

Pungashe fled to the protection of the powerful Ndwandwe chief, Zwide, Dingiswayo's greatest enemy. Zwide was surprised to hear that the young Zulu chief had been able to crush the Butelezi so thoroughly, but he had little patience or sympathy with losers, and quickly ordered Pungashe put to death.

Though the victory was his alone, Shaka claimed that he had been acting only as Dingiswayo's vassal. As was customary in such a situation, he offered Dingiswayo the captured cattle. Dingiswayo replied to the offer of cattle with unusual generosity, allowing

Shaka to keep almost all of the beasts he had captured from the Butelezi.

The captured Butelezi women, about one hundred of them, became Shaka's personal property. They formed the basis for the celebrated Zulu female regiments and for Shaka's own personal harem or seraglio. The women were divided into three groups. Two were quartered in military kraals, where they lived under the stern eye of some of Shaka's elderly women relatives, his maiden aunt, Mkabayi, and Senzangakona's first wife, Mkabi, who had once been kind to Nandi. Nandi herself was overseer of the third group of young women, the *Um-dlunkulu*—"those of the great house."

Ultimately Shaka established a huge harem—estimates run from a little over a thousand to five thousand. The seraglio women were especially chosen for their beauty, and Shaka boasted that he could recall the personal history of every one of them. Yet he announced quite early in his career that he would never marry. The women in his harem were always referred to as his "sisters," never as his wives.

Since Zulu warriors were forced to remain bachelors, Shaka must have felt he could do no less. But there was another reason, as well. Shaka said that if he had any sons they would eventually attempt to assassinate him and take the throne. To guard against this he would produce no children at all. "Two bulls cannot live in the same kraal" was the way he put it. Shaka could find ample justification for such fears in the history of the surrounding tribes. Dingiswayo himself had nearly assassinated his own father, and

Shaka surely would have killed his had he been given the opportunity.

It would be quite wrong to believe that either Shaka or his bachelor warriors led a thoroughly celibate life. On special occasions Shaka would temporarily release a regiment from its vows of celibacy —and at the same time would release a corresponding regiment of women. The warriors and the women were allowed to enjoy sexual contact in the traditional ways open to unmarried couples among the Zulus. Any pregnancies that resulted, however, were generally punished by death. But if Shaka were feeling lenient he might overlook the death penalty and allow the guilty parties to pay off their "crime" with a fine of cattle. Shaka undoubtedly enjoyed his own seraglio women in the same way. There is no authentic evidence that he ever fathered a child. There are, however, rumors that he personally killed any of the seraglio women who became pregnant.

Occasionally, single warriors or entire regiments that had reached the proper age and had distinguished themselves in battle were allowed to put on the headring and marry. They were usually given a large supply of cattle with which to start their own kraals. Thus, even the power to marry came under Shaka's control. It was simply another prize that he could offer his men if they fought bravely.

By 1817, approximately one year after Shaka became Zulu chief, he had quadrupled the amount of territory under his control. He now commanded an army of respectable size, containing about two thousand superbly trained warriors. But he still remained a loyal vassal of Dingiswayo to all outward appearances.

During the autumn of 1817 (autumn in the Southern Hemisphere begins in March), Shaka received word that his foster father Mbiya was dying. Shaka had a genuine affection for the old man and wanted to see him. He and a picked group of two hundred warriors covered the sixty miles between his home and Mbiya's kraal on the coast in a little over a day. When Shaka arrived, he found that Mbiya was already beyond hope. There was nothing to do except sacrifice a few oxen to insure a safe journey for the old man's spirit.

Just sixteen miles from where Mbiya lay dying was the Yengweni kraal, home of Dingiswayo. Much had changed since Dingiswayo and Shaka had last met, and there was a great deal to talk about, so a visit was arranged. Dingiswayo gave his favorite a warm reception and congratulated him on his many military successes. Then he explained to Shaka that Zulu aid would be needed in a campaign he was planning against Matiwane, chief of the powerful Ngwane tribe. Matiwane's land bordered that of an even more dangerous foe, Zwide, and Dingiswayo was anxious to have the Ngwane firmly under his control, so that they could act as a buffer against the growing power of Zwide and his Ndwandwe.

The campaign against Matiwane was to begin during the winter of 1817. Most long-term military operations in the area were carried out in winter. During the other seasons there were planting and harvesting and many other tasks to be performed at home. Besides, the weather was too hot and dry for the hard work of warfare except in winter.

From his own tribe and other vassals, Dingiswayo gathered about thirty-five hundred warriors. This did not represent the total strength he had available. For Dingiswayo, a cautious man, was unwilling to risk everything on the outcome of a single battle. He dispatched another two thousand of his own warriors to keep an eye on Zwide. Shaka was to supply one thousand Zulus for the attack.

A total force of about forty-five hundred marched across the White Umfolozi River against Matiwane in June of 1817. As later events were to demonstrate, Matiwane was a remarkably resourceful warrior, but he could offer no effective resistance to Dingiswayo, and he knew it. In expectation of defeat, Matiwane sent the bulk of his cattle away for safe-keeping among the Hlubi people of the north.

In the councils of war, Shaka argued for total warfare and complete destruction of the Ngwanes. Dingiswayo and his other *indunas* rejected the idea. Shaka's well-trained Zulus were to be used primarily to terrify the Ngwanes into a quick surrender, not to wipe them out.

After a few half-hearted attempts at defense, Matiwane accepted Dingiswayo's overlordship. He was given a lecture on obedience and the need to maintain peace and order. Then Dingiswayo and his army retired homeward. Shaka was furious. He pointed out that nothing had really changed and that Dingiswayo had made himself neither loved nor feared, thus gain-ing no real power. Such leniency, Shaka argued, would only embolden other ambitious men such as Zwide.

In fact that is exactly what happened. Zwide had been smarting over several past defeats suffered at the hands of Dingiswayo and was looking for a way to recover his damaged military reputation, as well as to gain land and cattle for his growing tribe. An obvious potential victim was Matiwane. The Ngwanes had just been defeated by Dingiswayo and did not have the strength to offer serious resistance. Matiwane was in particular trouble since the Hlubis refused to return the cattle he had sent to them for safe-keeping.

Zwide attacked the Ngwanes, and his warriors killed every Ngwane they could catch, driving the rest permanently from their homes. Matiwane now faced an agonizing choice: He could let his own people starve, or he could attack another tribe and take their land and cattle. Clearly he had the duty of keeping his people alive, so he led his desperate forces against the Hlubis. The Ngwanes, who were fighting for survival, showed little mercy in victory, treating the Hlubis to a taste of *impi ebomvu*.

A deadly game of dominoes had begun in southern Africa. Ultimately all of the southern Bantu tribes were to be convulsed by a series of migrations and wars unlike any they had experienced before. More than a million people died as a result of this upheaval, and the tribal structure of southern Africa was permanently shattered. These migrations and wars are usually attributed to the expansion of the Zulu empire under Shaka, and certainly Shaka contributed to them. But the conquests of the Zulus were not the only cause. It can also be argued that Zwide began the process with his savage attack on Matiwane. In any case the exact starting point is unimportant. The basic cause was that the Bantu had simply run out of room. In order to expand, the tribes now had to seize territory that was already inhabited by other tribes.

Dingiswayo was angered by Zwide's attack on Matiwane, for Matiwane had just become his vassal, and Dingiswayo was honor-bound to provide some sort of protection for him. Still, both Dingiswayo and Zwide were cautious about taking the final step toward war, though both prepared for it. The break finally came as a result of a complicated family feud in which Zwide killed Dingiswayo's son-in-law. Dingiswayo sent word to Shaka to organize an invasion of Ndwandwe territory. The plan was to attack Zwide's homeland from two sides and crush him between their forces.

It was an excellent strategy. The Ndwandwes could not possibly have resisted the combined forces of the Mtetwa and the Zulus. But two things went wrong. Shaka and the Zulus were delayed and did not cross into Ndwandwe territory at the scheduled time. Whether the delay was an accident, or whether Shaka deliberately held back his forces, hoping that Dingiswayo and Zwide would destroy one another, will never be known. To make the situation worse, Dingiswayo, unarmed and accompanied only by a few of his wives, wandered away from his army and was captured by Ndwandwe warriors.

It was said later that Dingiswayo had been captured through the use of witchcraft. All Bantu peoples believed in witchcraft and magic, and this belief was particularly strong in the Ndwandwe tribe. Zwide's mother, Ntombazi, was thought to be a powerful witch and kept the skulls of all the chiefs her son had killed on poles in her hut, a practice that was supposed to confer to the Ndwandwe the power that their owners had once possessed.

Zwide was almost overcome by his good luck in capturing Dingiswayo so easily. At first he didn't seem to know what to do about it. He feared that Dingiswayo had merely offered himself as a decoy in some sort of subtle trap. Zwide held Dingiswayo a prisoner but treated him with great courtesy. After a few days, however, he had The Great One executed. Dingiswayo's head became the proudest exhibit in Ntombazi's skull collection.

Bits and pieces of the great chief went into the cooking pots of various witch doctors, for it was believed that the flesh of such a man possessed powerful magical properties. What was left of his body was buried with all the honors due a mighty chief.

The women who had been captured with Dingiswayo killed themselves in grief. The Mtetwa army was so stricken by the loss of their leader that they simply melted away.

Dingiswayo, one of the most important chiefs of the Bantu peoples, had ruled less than ten years.

V

Dingiswayo's Heir

SHAKA ARRIVED LATE for the attack on Zwide only to discover that Dingiswayo was already dead and his army in full retreat. The Zulu chief's informants were members of the Kumalo, a small clan in Dingiswayo's empire. The Ndwandwe now so far outnumbered the Zulus that any thought of an attack by Shaka's forces alone was out of the question. He and his army retired quickly and quietly. Shaka may well have owed his life to the timely information supplied by the Kumalo, and he never forgot them.

Dingiswayo's death left a vacuum among the Nguni peoples. One of his half brothers succeeded him to the Mtetwa throne but was unable to control the tribes. Without Dingiswayo himself, the Mtetwa could no longer exercise supremacy over their subjects.

Zwide was the leading contender to become heir to Dingiswayo's power. The skill of Shaka's army, if not its size, made the Zulus, too, a factor in the contest. The Qwabe and the Tembu, both strong and ambitious tribes, were also to play a part in the coming struggle.

For a year following Dingiswayo's death there was a great deal of jockeying for position. The Zulus found themselves in an uncomfortable spot, for their territory lay in the middle of all the other contenders. Zwide tried to form an alliance with the Qwabe and the Tembu, holding out as a prize the land of the Zulus, which was to be divided among the three tribes. Simultaneously Shaka was trying to coax the Qwabe and Tembu into an alliance with him by frightening them with tales of Zwide's treachery to his neighbors, and by warning them that Zwide was "The Eater-up of Chiefs." The Qwabe and the Tembu decided not to give their support to either side, probably hoping that Zwide and Shaka would destroy one another.

Only the territory of the little Kumalo clan lay between Zwide and Shaka. Zwide was angry at the Kumalo for having informed Shaka of Dingiswayo's death and the retreat of his army. In revenge, he exterminated the older leaders of the clan and picked Mzilikazi, son of an executed chief, to rule over the remaining Kumalo.

Zwide believed that Mzilikazi would be an obedient puppet, but Mzilikazi knew he would survive only as long as Zwide needed him and that there was no telling how long that might be. He fled to Shaka's protection, where he was warmly received.

Zwide felt that he could easily defeat the Zulus, and his confidence seemed well founded. Though the skill of Shaka's armies was widely known, Zwide had at least twice the number of warriors at his command, and the Ndwandwe were redoubtable fighters. In early April 1818, Zwide's host advanced into Zululand. The army itself was led by Nomahlanjana, Zwide's son and heir, and many of Zwide's other grown sons accompanied the force. Zwide himself, who was about fifty years old, never traveled with his army.

Shaka had developed an extensive intelligence-gathering system, and his spies kept him well informed concerning the size and progress of the Ndwandwe army. The Zulu chief always preferred to launch an attack, ravaging someone else's land, rather than to stand and defend his own. But in this case he had no choice. The Zulus were so thoroughly outnumbered that they could not use their "encircling horns." The Ndwandwes had not yet adopted Zulu fighting tactics, but they were familiar with them, so Shaka could not hope that the enemy would be shattered with one well-placed charge. Shaka's best chance lay in finding a good defensive position and allowing the Ndwandwes to exhaust themselves with fruitless attacks against his well-disciplined lines.

The main Zulu force was therefore concentrated atop Qokli hill, a high, conical hill with a circular depression at the summit. Shaka hoped to hide part of his army in this depression so that the Ndwandwes would be deceived as to the strength of the force they were attacking. Another important factor in Shaka's choice of location was that the hill was far from any available water. The Zulu troops at the top had carried ample supplies of water with them. Shaka knew that during the course of the battle the Ndwandwe warriors would become thirsty and would be forced to seek out water.

Even if the battle went against the Zulus, Shaka believed that they could hold out until nightfall and then cut their way through the surrounding forces and escape into a nearby forest.

Shaka employed a number of other stratagems to reduce the Ndwandwe numerical superiority as much as possible. Before arriving at Qokli hill, the Ndwandwes had to cross a swift river. Shaka posted guards at all the possible crossing spots. The Zulus knew that they could not hold back the Ndwandwes for long, but Shaka's guards took a terrible toll of enemy warriors as they tried to wade through the water. Only a dozen or so Zulus were killed, while several hundred Ndwandwes lost their lives in this part of the operation.

After the Ndwandwes had crossed the river they saw a large number of Zulu cattle being driven off in the distance. The Ndwandwe commander sent about a third of his men in pursuit of the Zulu herds, thinking that a large part of the Zulu army would be protecting the valuable cattle. In fact, the herds were guarded by only a small detachment. Shaka had reasoned that by the time the cattle were captured and brought back, the main battle at the hill would already have been decided, and a large section of the Ndwandwe army would not have been able to participate.

Shaka knew that his only real hope for victory lay in the superior training and discipline of his own troops. Before the battle he harangued them on the need to keep their ranks closed and to maintain silence so that they could hear the commands shouted by their leaders. Most of all, he warned the Zulus to beware of any simulated retreat by the Ndwandwes. This was an old battle trick by which the Ndwandwes attempted to lure their opponents out of a defensible position. Shaka warned that any man who broke ranks and ran more than half a spear's throw ahead of his formation, no matter how heroic he might be, would be executed.

Nomahlanjana, the Ndwandwe commander, received reports from his spies indicating that the hill was held by only a small Zulu force. Shaka's ruse of concealing a portion of his army at the top had worked well.

Nomahlanjana expected an easy victory. He ordered the hill surrounded and attacked from all sides. Then he sat down under a tree to await news of the inevitable result.

As the Ndwandwe force advanced up all sides of the hill, the Zulus remained seated, looking at them with apparent indifference. Then, on a command from Shaka, the front line of defenders rose as one man. The Zulus were to become famous for their precision mass movements. Each of the fifteen hundred warriors struck his right foot on the ground and beat his spear against his shield for a few seconds. It was an impressive and ominous demonstration. Quite suddenly the Zulus looked much more formidable than they had when seated.

The Ndwandwes hurled their assegais and closed in on the Zulu defenders at the top of the hill. In doing so, they made a serious tactical mistake. They charged up the hill in closely packed ranks. As their front lines tightened into an ever-smaller circle, the Ndwandwe warriors began to get into one another's way. There was not even enough room for them to hurl a spear properly.

That was what Shaka had waited for. He ordered the front line of Zulus to charge the packed and confused Ndwandwe ranks.

After about ten minutes of hand-to-hand combat there was a lull, and the Ndwandwe warriors retired to the bottom of the hill. Both sides assessed their losses. Ndwandwe's dead outnumbered the Zulu dead at least three to one. The Ndwandwe tried another charge, this time spacing their lines farther apart to avoid the crush at the top. But the results were not much better; the Zulus inflicted grave losses on them once again.

Midday was approaching, and the Ndwandwe were beginning to suffer the effects of thirst. While the Zulu warriors were able to drink from their ample stores, large segments of the Ndwandwe army were forced to wander off in search of water. Zulu preparation was paying off in another way, as well. Lightly wounded Zulu warriors were provided with bandages made of bark and sent back into the lines to fight. The gravely wounded, and all captured enemy wounded were, as usual, killed.

Nomahlanjana began to view his badly mauled forces with alarm. He still had far more warriors than the Zulus, but his superiority had been greatly diminished, and the charges up the hill were clearly not helping his position. A simulated retreat failed to break Zulu discipline. Worse still, the barefoot Zulus chased his men so speedily that the feigned retreat nearly turned into a rout.

After a discussion with his commanders, Nomahlanjana decided to stake everything on a battering-ram charge. A heavy column of warriors was sent up the south side of Qokli hill. The hope was that a strong charge would drive the tired Zulu defenders back into a semicircle of Ndwandwes who were surrounding the bottom of the north side of the hill.

As the Ndwandwe column charged up the hill they were astonished to see two columns of completely fresh Zulu warriors racing toward them. These columns outflanked the Ndwandwe force and circled around behind it. Shaka had finally thrown his hidden reserves into battle, enabling him to use his favorite encircling "horns" maneuver.

The Ndwandwe troops in the semicircle on the north side of the hill awaited what they confidently expected would be a panic-stricken stream of Zulus fleeing into the trap that had been set for them. They could not see what was happening on the other side of the hill. Only when survivors appeared, most of them seriously wounded, did they learn that the trap had actually been set by Shaka and that the Ndwandwes had run straight into it. The main column had been destroyed, and five sons of Zwide, including Nomahlanjana himself, had been cut down in the disastrous charge. Moreover, Shaka had sent his swift, barefooted killers to the nearby springs to butcher all the stragglers who had wandered off in search of water.

Still, the battle was not over. Shaka had arranged for a series of smoke signals from his scouts so that he could be informed of the movements of the Ndwandwe force that had been sent out in pursuit of the Zulu cattle. These warriors had caught up with the herds and had easily captured them from the small Zulu contingent that was guarding them. Now the Ndwandwe were returning to Qokli hill with the Zulu cattle. Once they joined up with the remaining Ndwandwe they would constitute a dangerous fighting force, especially since most of the cattle chasers were relatively fresh, while the Zulus had many casualties and were tired from a long day of fighting. Shaka decided it was time to abandon the hill and withdrew to the vicinity of the royal kraal.

The Ndwandwe followed, but they were badly slowed by the huge herd of Zulu cattle, which they were unwilling to abandon. Their slowness may have cost them a victory. While they moved along at a leisurely pace, the Zulus were able to reach Bulawayo safely and to muster those warriors who had been left to guard the royal kraal. The Zulus were also reinforced by warriors who had returned from slaughtering the Ndwandwe stragglers at the springs. As a result the Ndwandwe felt they could not risk another open battle and turned homeward, taking most of the

Zulu cattle with them. The Zulus, exhausted from the day's fighting, dared not pursue.

The battle of Qokli hill was not a complete Zulu victory, but in assessing the day's results, Shaka could be satisfied. He had lost most of his cattle, but his warriors had fought magnificently, beating back an attack by a much larger force. The casualty figures show the extent of the Zulu accomplishment. Some seventy-five hundred Ndwandwes were killed, including five princes. Zulu losses amounted to fifteen hundred killed and five hundred seriously wounded. Still, the losses in both cattle and men had hurt the Zulus.

Shaka realized that the battle of Qokli hill had not ended the Ndwandwe threat. A large portion of Zwide's army had retreated intact, and the king could summon additional strength from dependent tribes to his north. But Zwide would think twice about attacking the Zulus again. That would give Shaka time, and time was what he needed. After the battle of Qokli hill, the Zulus could probably not have put more than two thousand unwounded warriors into the field. Yet the engagement had so enhanced the prestige of Zulu arms that Shaka's ranks were flooded with adventurers and warriors from many different tribes and clans.

All the warriors to enter the Zulu army, regardless of their original tribe or clan, were treated equally. They were assigned to regiments according to their age. There they mixed with warriors from many different backgrounds. Anyone could rise in the army if he served Shaka with fanatical devotion. Newcomers

were often able to advance above true-born Zulus and
even attain more power than members of the Zulu
royal family. Shaka made a policy of choosing his
commanders or military *indunas* from among com-
moners. These men owed their position entirely to
him and were apt to be loyal. Also, no matter how
powerful a military *induna* might become, he was un-
likely to turn into a potential rebel, because as a com-
moner, he could not call upon his fellow tribesmen to
follow him.

One of those to receive an early promotion was a
man called Ndlela (The Road), a former cannibal.
Cannibalism (except in certain specific ritual situa-
tions) was regarded with loathing by the Zulus. Can-
nibals were thought of as being inferior and unclean.
Yet Ndlela advanced quickly in the Zulu military
service, and after Shaka's death his successor appointed Ndlela to the position of Chief *Induna*, a
sort of prime minister. The Zulu ruler never acted
without at least going through the motions of con-
sulting Ndlela.

The system of age regiments imposed by Shaka did
more than improve the fighting efficiency of the Zulu
army; it also went a long way toward changing the
nature of Zulu society. Clansmen were scattered into
many different military kraals. They were no longer
led by men of their own clan. As a result, anyone who
entered Shaka's service began to assume the right to
call himself a Zulu. Whereas Dingiswayo had been
content to allow local chiefs to rule their own people
as they wished, Shaka was determined to break up the
conquered tribes and mold them into a single Zulu
nation.

Shaka made few exceptions to the practice of breaking up the old clan and tribal aggregations. One of these exceptions involved Mzilikazi, the Kumalo chieftain who had fled from Zwide to the protection of the Zulus. Shaka gave Mzilikazi a high position in the Zulu army, and most of the warriors under his command were members of his own clan. Mzilikazi was therefore able to reassert his chieftainship over the Kumalo with Shaka's blessing. Just why Shaka allowed Mzilikazi such unaccustomed freedom is not clear. Perhaps at this early stage in his career, he felt he had no choice. Whatever his reasons, he was later to regret the decision.

Shaka had undoubtedly always planned to make himself the total ruler of the Zulus, a monarch unhampered by the traditional restraints placed upon the ordinary Bantu king or chief. Everything he did, from the moment he mounted the Zulu throne, seems to indicate that he was operating with a well-ordered plan in mind. But during his early years as Zulu chief he had to move carefully, for there were powerful forces that might seek to overthrow him if he made a misstep.

One of the most powerful independent forces among the Zulu, indeed among all Bantu tribes, were those individuals who dealt with the supernatural: the wizards, witch doctors, and witch finders. Belief in and fear of witchcraft among the Bantu were overwhelming and unquestioned facts of life. Practically every major event—birth, death, planting, harvest, preparation for war, or the installation of a new chief—was accompanied by elaborate magical rituals. These were of two types. First there were rituals to enlist the aid of magical powers for success or happiness. Second, and perhaps more important, there were rituals aimed at warding off the spells and enchantments of the *umtakati,* the evildoers or wizards.

Belief in witchcraft was based upon fear. To the Zulus there was no such thing as an accident. Any unfortunate event, from a bad harvest to an illness, was blamed on the activities of the *umtakati.* The evildoers were believed to be able to hide their guilty secrets in an innocent guise. They might even be unaware of the evil forces that they generated. *Umtakati* might be ordinary men or they might be quite prominent. No one except the king himself was safe from suspicion. When a dire event, particularly the illness of a king, befell a community, the witch doctors and witch finders, the *isangomas,* were summoned to find the guilty parties in a rite called a "smelling out" —a uniquely descriptive term.

The *isangomas,* who were usually women, exercised a great deal of power. Though they were supposed to guard the tribe from evil, the *isangomas* were feared and hated by ordinary people. Like the hangmen of Europe, they were considered necessary, but few cared to associate with them. The *isangomas* lived almost as outcasts on the fringes of the tribe, but this distance tended to increase the fearfulness of their reputation. Once an *isangoma* laid on a man her fly whisk, made from the tail of a gnu, that man was doomed. There was no appeal, and the punishment was a particularly horrible sort of death called skewering. Sharp stakes were driven up the victim's rectum, and he was left to expire slowly in agony.

Before one too quickly denounces the savagery of the Bantu, it would be well to remember what European witch hunters did to their victims. Civilization has never improved the humanity of witch hunters. It has merely led to more sophisticated means of torturing victims. The Bantu believed that any form of extended imprisonment or torture was inhuman. Their usual punishment for a crime was a quick death. The fact that most peoples have reserved their most horrible punishments for those accused of being witches indicates that witchcraft has been almost universally considered the vilest and most dangerous of crimes. Punishment for witchcraft, therefore, often exceeds the bounds generally deemed by a particular people to be proper.

But the Bantu institution of witch hunting was not supported solely by fear of the supernatural. If the condemned man was a kraal head, as he usually was, all his wives and children would also be executed, though more mercifully. Then his kraal would be burned down and all his cattle given to the chief. The chief might subsequently distribute the cattle among his favorites.

The witch finders were thus in a position to exercise a good deal of control over the internal politics of a tribe. The condemnation of a rich man might be heartily approved by the chief and his supporters, because they would profit directly from it. Anyone who was unpopular or who was thought to be dangerous could easily be disposed of during a "smelling out."

Many chiefs also used the *isangomas* to get rid of possible rivals and troublemakers.

Although the *isangomas* might be useful to a chief, they could not be completely controlled, and their wishes always had to be taken into account. They represented a conservative and traditional force in the tribe, a force that resisted radical innovations and stood ready to exterminate anyone who rose above the level attained by his fellow tribesmen. For the type of state that Shaka was building, such a major counterforce to his own power could not be tolerated indefinitely. The grip of the *isangoma* over the Zulu people had to be broken, and the supernatural forces they were believed to control placed entirely in the hands of Shaka himself.

Because Shaka conducted a long and vigorous campaign against the witch doctors, some have believed that he was skeptical about the power of witchcraft itself. This hardly seems likely. Throughout his career Shaka took elaborate, almost fanatical measures to guard himself against the *umtakati,* and he carefully attended to all the magical rituals of the Zulus.

Shaka sincerely believed in witchcraft, but he certainly doubted the powers and the honesty of the *isangoma*. This apparent contradiction is not an unusual one. European history contains many examples of Christian kings who persecuted priests and even went to war against the pope, yet still considered themselves to be good and devout Catholics.

Early in Shaka's reign the appearance of a number of evil omens prompted a general "smelling out." This was a dramatic and terrifying event, for none of those

who attended, except Shaka himself, could be sure
that he would emerge alive. An accused man had
only one hope of survival. If he was quick enough to
reach the feet of the king he might claim sanctuary,
and if Shaka granted this, the proceedings against
him were at an end. But this did not happen often,
for *isangomas* were closely followed by the slayers,
muscular professional killers whose duty it was to seize
the condemned man and immediately drag him off to
his execution. Furthermore, the "smelling out" ceremony was such an overwhelmingly terrifying experience that the condemned were usually paralyzed by
panic and unable to resist. Belief in witchcraft ran so
deep that many accused persons felt they really were
guilty and deserved death, though they had been unaware of their guilt until the moment that the *isangoma's* gnu-tailed switch touched their shoulder. The
same acceptance of guilt was common among those
who were accused of witchcraft in Europe.

For the "smelling out" all adult males were gathered in front of Shaka at Bulawayo. After a few
moments of tension the five grotesquely dressed *isangomas* rushed among the crowd shrieking and
screaming. E. A. Ritter, a South African writer, has
reconstructed this picture of a Zulu *isangoma:*

"Her face was an evil mask streaked with white
clay paint, which also covered her arms and legs. An
assortment of dried and inflated bladders and snake-
skins adorned her head and arms. Claws and teeth of
leopards and hyaenas and goats' horns hung from her
neck, and over her shrunken breasts grinned the skulls
of two baboons. A kilt of softened cowhide hung from

her hips to above her knees. In her hand she carried
the tail of a gnu or wildebeest, which resembled that
of a horse."

As the witch finders threaded their way through
the crowd, the people chanted. This chanting often
guided the *isangoma* in making accusations that would
be popular with the tribe. When the *isangoma* approached an individual who was widely disliked the
chanting might grow louder, while when she seemed
about to accuse someone who was well regarded, the
chanting would die away. The witch finders were
generally too clever to attempt to make an accusation
that would be resented by the entire community.

At his first "smelling out" Shaka warned the *isangomas* to make no accusations against any of his
military *indunas*. When they did so anyway, he immediately granted the *indunas* sanctuary and proclaimed that if the witch finders did not withdraw
their accusations they would be executed with their
own skewers. The accusations were withdrawn.

Shaka moved with unusual deliberation and caution
against the *isangomas*. Under ordinary circumstances,
the mere nod of his head was enough to send any
number of persons to their deaths, for no reason other
than that Shaka desired it. But in the case of the
witch finders he was forced, at first, to threaten and
bargain. Shortly after the first "smelling out" Shaka
placed all Zulu warriors, not merely the *indunas,*
beyond the power of the *isangomas*.

Another major power in the tribe were the elders.
Though the old men held no "legal" position—that
is there was no area in which their decisions were

final—they wielded considerable authority in most tribes, and their approval was generally sought in any important undertaking. Like the witch finders, they were a conservative influence on the tribe. They were always ready to uphold the traditional ways and opposed innovations. Shaka, who was intent on breaking traditions and ruling without restraint, dealt with the elders early in his career.

Breaking the power of the elders proved to be remarkably easy. The old men could not fight, and in the increasingly militaristic Zulu state they began to appear useless. When Shaka took the Zulu throne he refused to treat the elders as venerable authorities. Rather, he derided them as "old women." To subject the elders to the ridicule of his warriors, Shaka compelled the elders to wear petticoats of monkey skins that resembled the garments worn by old women.

Zulus composed songs to commemorate all sorts of events. Shaka, who was an excellent songster, is said to have composed one that contained these lines:

> The aged must be separated and placed in the rear
>> Do you not see they impede the King's army?
> They were men formerly,
>> But now our mother's Mothers
> We must find them petticoats to wear

By the time the Ndwandwe were defeated, the elders had fallen into such disrepute and Shaka's personal power had grown so great, that he was able to order the execution of a large number of this once-important group. He even named one of his royal kraals Gibixegu, which means "Drive Out the Old

Men." The surviving elders had no power with which to oppose the wishes of the king.

While gradually changing the life of his people Shaka also continued his conquests of neighboring tribes. The defeat of the Ndwandwe freed the Zulu army to undertake campaigns against weaker tribes. In mid-1818 the Zulus attacked the large Qwabe tribe, which had once attempted to straddle the fence between Shaka and Zwide. The defeat of the Qwabe forces was quick and complete. The Qwabe chief, Pakatwayo, died in convulsions after hearing of the destruction of his army. However, there was a strong suspicion that the convulsions had been caused not by humiliation but by poison administered by disappointed relatives. Shaka used the incident as an excuse to execute most of the members of the Qwabe royal family and to expropriate the royal cattle and the royal harem.

Shaka did not incorporate the entire Qwabe tribe into his own but allowed them to live under the leadership of the dead chief's brother, Nqetho. Nqetho pledged fealty to Shaka and for as long as the Zulu king lived, remained completely loyal; indeed, he became Shaka's trusted friend. But the Qwabe, as a semi-independent chiefdom, represented a potential danger to the future of the Zulu empire.

Shaka had begun with a tiny clan and about a hundred square miles of territory. Two and one-half years after he assumed the throne, he was the absolute ruler of seven thousand square miles, from the White Umfolozi River in the north to the Tugela River in the south, and from the Indian Ocean to the

Nkandla Forest in the west. Shaka had conquered thirty chiefs and their clans. Most of these people were now considered Zulus, owing complete and unquestioning obedience to Shaka.

Zwide had watched with concern as his rival's strength grew. The Ndwandwe chief levied more troops from the Swazi clans to the north who were under his control. He had all his soldiers trained in Zulu tactics and in the use of Zulu weapons. In May 1819, a Ndwandwe army eighteen thousand strong crossed the White Umfolozi into Shaka's domain.

Shaka was ready for the invasion. He had cleared a forty-mile-wide swath south of the White Umfolozi of all cattle and grain. There was nothing in this invasion corridor that the Ndwandwe could steal. It was customary for the Bantu armies—indeed, for all armies up to this time—to carry only a few days' worth of food supplies and then live off the land, taking grain from farmers and cattle from herdsmen. For this reason invasions were usually disastrously destructive, even if they ended in a small battle or no battle at all. Armies proceeded like a plague of locusts, devouring everything in their path. The Ndwandwe army was a force of almost unprecedented size in black Africa, and they had brought few supplies with them. Shaka led the enemy on into the desolated region by sending a small, highly mobile body of troops to lay a false trail and to harass them.

For a week the huge Ndwandwe army chased the Zulus, all the while getting hungrier and hungrier.

Even hunting provided little, for the Zulus had driven most of the wild game out of the area.

The Ndwandwe commander, Soshangane, finally decided that he could no longer continue the fruitless chase. He marched his army into the Nkandla Forest, where he hoped they would find enough food to make their long retreat home without undue hardship.

Shaka had no intention of allowing the Ndwandwe army to escape intact, for he knew that they would be back again, and next time he might not be as well prepared. The first night the Ndwandwes were camped in the forest, Shaka sent out a small raiding party to infiltrate the enemy. There was little dry wood for fires, so the Ndwandwe army slept in almost total darkness. The Zulus crept into the Ndwandwe camp and began stabbing sleeping warriors.

The screams of wounded men immediately awakened the rest of the army. In the gloom, the Zulu killers were indistinguishable from Ndwandwe warriors, and when the Ndwandwes began to shout out questions about what had happened, the Zulus joined in.

Then one of the Zulus screamed that he had just seen a wizard riding on a hyena (the most fearful sort of wizard), and the rumor spread that the killings had been accomplished by witchcraft. The Ndwandwe warriors did not fear death by ordinary means, but they feared witchcraft. The gloomy forest, quite unlike the open land in which they normally lived, had already made them uneasy. Now the mysterious deaths, coupled with the talk of witchcraft, created

a near panic. It was only with difficulty that Soshangane was able to calm his troops.

The exhausted Ndwandwes again tried to sleep,
but there was another wave of mysterious killings in
the darkness. The Ndwandwes began striking out
blindly, killing one another in their panic. During the
confusion, the Zulu infiltrators escaped and returned
to Shaka to report the dramatic success of their mission.

Early next morning the Ndwandwe army marched
out of the forest under the watchful eyes of Shaka's
scouts. The warriors were hungry, exhausted from a
sleepless night, and thoroughly demoralized. Though
Ndwandwe leaders had guessed that it was Zulus and
not witchcraft that had caused the mysterious deaths,
the warriors themselves remained unconvinced. Since
the beginning of the expedition, they had been dogged
by such unusual bad luck that they believed it could
be due only to supernatural influences. A feeling of
doom hung over the retreating army. Shaka decided
that the moment had come to attack.

Although no battle had yet been fought, the
Ndwandwes had already lost some two thousand men
through death or desertion. This still left them with
a considerable manpower advantage, for they had
sixteen thousand warriors to the Zulus' ten thousand.
But when the Zulus attacked, it was all the tired and
dispirited Ndwandwes could do to hold down their
losses and continue their retreat in good order.

For two full days there were repeated skirmishes.
Finally, while the Ndwandwes were attempting to
cross a river, a massive Zulu charge managed to crack

the enemy's discipline. The once-proud army broke up into little bands of panicky fugitives. Hard on their heels were the barefooted Zulu killers, who were becoming experts at tracking and slaughtering.

The Ndwandwe territory now lay open and defenseless. Zwide had retained no adequate home guard, for he could not imagine that his great army would be so completely shattered. Shaka gathered his freshest and fastest troops and sent them directly to Zwide's royal kraal to capture the king and his infamous mother, who had kept the museum of skulls. In a single day that Zulu column covered seventy miles.

As they approached Zwide's kraal, the Zulus sang the Ndwandwe victory song in order to trick the king into thinking that it was his own army returning in victory. But as they came closer the Zulus began to slaughter the women and children who rushed out to greet them. Zwide was alerted to the ruse, and with two of his sons he managed to escape into the darkness.

At daybreak the Zulu army swept through Ndwandwe territory, killing every human being it encountered and capturing every cow, goat, and sheep. All kraals and fields were burned. Ndwandwe land was turned into a virtual desert.

The prize prisoner of the second Ndwandwe war was Ntombazi, Zwide's mother. According to Zulu legend, Shaka had her executed by imprisoning her with a hungry hyena, which chewed her up bit by bit.

Zwide fled northward, putting at least two hundred miles between himself and the victorious Zulus. He had been a great chief, and even in defeat his influence was considerable. Ndwandwe refugees flocked to join him, and he began to build up a new army with which to oppose the Zulus. But it was a process that would take many years, and before it could be accomplished, Zwide seems to have run afoul of the chieftainess who ruled the small Bapodi clan. This clan had been protected by the inaccessible valley in which they dwelt and by their leader's well-established reputation as a powerful sorceress. It is said that this formidable woman's magic was directed against Zwide, who died shortly afterward. The exact date and circumstances of Zwide's death are unknown.

Another section of the Ndwandwe followed Soshangane northward into territory that had been held by the Portuguese. Soshangane drove the Portuguese out and founded a realm that was beyond the reach of the Zulu *impis*. It was known as the Empire of Gaza. Still a third group of Ndwandwes under a leader called Zwangendaba also fled northward, embarking on a migration that took them past Lake Tanganyika.

Shaka ordered a great victory celebration and allowed some of his older regiments to put on their headrings and marry. Younger warriors were still bound to remain bachelors, but for a few days they were released from their obligation to remain celibate. Corresponding female regiments were also released and were allowed to engage in the traditional Zulu premarital sexual activity. If any pregnancies resulted, the warrior responsible was asked only to pay a fine in cattle. Shaka was in an expansive mood.

The year was 1820. Shaka had extended his domain north to the Pongola River and westward to the Blood River. This region was to be known as Zululand, and was to remain the heart of Shaka's empire, though the area under his direct control increased greatly in the years to come. Under his command were thousands of the finest warriors in Africa and a nation of a quarter of a million people, most of whom called themselves Zulus.

1. A typical Bantu kraal.

2. Bantu and their cattle.

3. A Zulu blacksmith at work. From a painting by George French Angas made about 1848.

4. Shaka, king of the Zulus. Though this drawing was made during Shaka's lifetime, it may be highly romanticized.

5. A composite painting of Shaka by Captain A. D. Shorey. The painting was made after a careful study of photographs of Shaka's living relatives.

6. A Zulu hunting dance. From a painting by George French Angas made about 1848.

7. Zulu warriors. From a painting by George French Angas made about 1848.

8. Henry Francis Fynn.

9. A Zulu dance.

10. Shaka's *indunas* conducting a parley. This drawing appeared in the *Illustrated London News* in 1902.

11. Shaka's half brother, murderer, and successor, Dingane.

VI

Shaka's Court

BEFORE 1824 SHAKA had probably never seen a white man. He had heard of them, of course, and was aware of the danger represented by their firearms. But the settlement nearest to Bulawayo was the little Portuguese colony at Delagoa Bay. The larger settlements of the Cape Colony were still too distant to be of any danger or of much interest to the Zulu monarch. European expansion in southern Africa had not yet begun in earnest.

While Shaka was building his empire, some English traders were considering the possibility of opening up the region called Natal for trade and future settlement. Natal was the area lying roughly between the Portuguese settlements and the colonies of the Cape. Much of this land was part of the Zulu empire, but the British traders were most interested in the territory south of the Tugela River, which lay south of the

Zulu heartland. Shaka's *impis* were in the process of putting this region under his complete control at just about the time the whites were thinking of settling there. The white men knew nothing of Shaka and the Zulus. They expected Natal to be occupied by small tribes and clans, just as the rest of southern Africa was.

In 1823 the brig *Salisbury* sailed up the coast of Natal looking for a possible place to found a British settlement. At the Bay of St. Lucia two small boats were put out to try for a landing. They capsized in the heavy surf, and six men drowned. Among the survivors was Francis George Farewell, leader of the effort to found a Natal settlement. Farewell owed his life to Jakot Msimbiti, a Xhosa prisoner who had picked up some English and a little Dutch from his contact with white men at the Cape. Jakot also spoke several Bantu dialects.

At the Cape, Jakot had been arrested as a cattle thief and then forced to serve as an interpreter instead of being sent to a penal colony. Jakot (who is usually referred to as Jacob) was a remarkably good swimmer and helped to pull Farewell through the surf, but another of the survivors accused him of deliberately upsetting the boats. Having already been treated badly by white men, Jakot seized the first opportunity to escape from them and take his chances with the tribes of the interior.

Farewell was eventually rescued from the coast and returned to the Cape Colony, his enthusiasm for the Natal venture undimmed. The following year, the Farewell Trading Company sent a party of thirty under the leadership of Henry Francis Fynn to Port Natal (now Durban, South Africa).

At the time, Fynn was just thirty years old, but he had already lived in Africa for a number of years and was reasonably knowledgeable about it. He had even made an effort to learn some of the Bantu languages. Though he was then little more than an adventurer, he had a genuine interest in Africa, an unusual quality for an Englishman of his day, even an Englishman in Africa. Fynn may have heard the name Shaka before he came to Natal, but the extent of the Zulu king's empire was quite unknown to him.

The inhabitants of the Port Natal region were members of the small Tuli clan, but none were to be seen when Fynn and his party went ashore. The Tuli had been subjected to almost continuous Zulu cattle raids. One day they became exasperated and attacked a Zulu patrol. Much to their surprise they wiped out the Zulus. Since that time the Tuli had lived in fear of Shaka's retribution. They had abandoned their fields and cattle herds and had taken to the wilderness, where they existed as best they could, sometimes resorting to cannibalism.

Seeing Fynn and his armed followers as possible protection against the Zulus, the Tuli began creeping out of their hiding places. It was from these terrified refugees that Fynn first learned that the land he was proposing to colonize was considered the personal property of the most powerful monarch in black Africa. Fynn decided that the wisest course was to negotiate directly with Shaka himself. Accompanied by his two Hottentot servants, Michael and John,

Fynn started out for Bulawayo, which he believed to
be only a few miles from Port Natal. Despite what he
had been told, Fynn could not imagine the existence
of a large Bantu empire. In fact, Shaka's kraal was
120 miles from Port Natal.

Fynn and his two servants began walking northward along the beach. They had traveled about
twelve miles when they became aware of a pounding
sound rising above the rhythmical noise of the surf.
The source of the sound turned out to be thousands
of pairs of feet running along the beach. An enormous
column of Zulu warriors was apparently chasing Fynn
and his servants. The Hottentots immediately headed
inland to hide in the forest, leaving the astonished and
frightened Fynn alone to greet the Zulu *indunas* leading the column. The Zulus were quite surprised to see
a white man in Natal, but they decided he was harm-
less enough and trotted on by with barely a backward
glance. Fynn tried to count the passing Zulus. When
he estimated twenty thousand, he could not believe his
own count, for as far as he knew, an army of such size
was inconceivable in Bantu Africa. Yet this was only
a part of Shaka's army. The Zulus had been on campaign in the south and were returning to Bulawayo.

Michael and John came out of their hiding places
and joined Fynn, who was now more anxious than
ever to see Shaka. The three followed the Zulu force,
and from kraal to kraal the word went forward that a
white man was coming to see Shaka. When Fynn had
nearly reached Bulawayo, however, a message was
sent back that Shaka was not yet ready to meet the
white man. The messengers told Fynn to return to

Port Natal and await the king's summons. Shaka sent along a gift of ivory and a few cattle, for he wished his message to be interpreted in the friendliest manner possible. He simply wanted time to find out more about the white man.

As Fynn returned to Port Natal, Shaka's spies followed him. They reported that the Port Natal colony contained only a handful of white men, who represented no threat. So Shaka invited all of them to visit him at Bulawayo. Seven white men and two Hottentots set out for the royal kraal on horseback. They had no idea what sort of reception they would receive.

As the horsemen passed through Zulu country, they were struck by how different the kraals appeared from those in other parts of southern Africa. The Zulu kraals were neat and almost compulsively orderly, contrasting sharply with the disorder of most Bantu kraals. The Zulus themselves displayed no particular interest in the white men; indeed, their indifference seemed to border upon arrogance.

The greatest surprise of all was Shaka's royal kraal. The outer fence was at least three miles in circumference. Inside was a vast circle of huts, at least fifteen hundred of them. The central cattle pen, or parade ground, was a mile in diameter, and as the riders approached they saw that it was jammed with people. Fynn estimated that eighty thousand people were in or around the kraal.

The riders were ordered to gallop around the kraal in a display of horsemanship and then to dismount and enter. When they came into the center of the kraal they found themselves in the midst of a dense

crowd of warriors, all in full regalia. At first there was
no way of telling who the king was, or even if he was
in the kraal at all. One of the *indunas* was delivering
a long speech, and the visitors were instructed to shout
"*yebo* [yes]" at every pause, though they hadn't the
slightest notion of what was being said.

During the speech Fynn was able to pick out Shaka
by his great height and by the respect showed to
him. Fynn pointed out the king to Farewell, and
Shaka noticed the two staring at him. He seemed delighted that he could be so easily recognized, even by
strangers, and he grinned and waggled a finger at his
guests.

Fynn recorded that when the speech and exchange
of gifts were over, Shaka "then raised the stick in his
hand and after striking it right and left and springing
out from amidst the chiefs, the whole mass broke
from their position and formed up into regiments.
Portions of these rushed to the river and the surrounding hills, while the remainder, forming themselves
into a circle, commenced dancing with Shaka, in their
midst. It was a most exciting scene, surprising to us,
who could not have imagined that a nation termed
'savages' could be so well disciplined. Regiments of
girls, headed by officers of their own sex, then entered the center of the arena to the number of 8,000
to 10,000, each holding a slight staff in her hand.
They joined in the dance, which continued for about
two hours. Shaka now came toward us, evidently seek-
ing our applause."

Farewell noticed one man who often stood by
Shaka's side and whispered to him. This man's face

was familiar. It was Jakot, the interpreter who had saved his life and then run off into the bush the year before.

Farewell knew that Jakot had no reason to love white men and feared that he might influence Shaka to have them killed. But the fears were groundless. Jakot did indeed hate white men, but at the moment he also needed them. After his escape he had made his way to Zulu territory, where his tales of the white men soon brought him to Shaka's attention. Shaka renamed him Hlabamanzi (The Swimmer) in honor of his feat of rescuing himself and Farewell. The Swimmer now held the unofficial position of Shaka's interpreter and adviser on white men. If the white men were killed, Jakot would no longer have a function.

Shaka had no intention of executing Farewell's party. He wanted to find out all he could about them, impress them with his wealth and with the power of the Zulus, and use them to his own advantage when he could.

As Fynn later described it, Shaka's costume must have been splendid: "Round his bare head he wore a circlet of stuffed otter skin, bearing within its circumference bunches of gorgeous red loury plumes and erect in front a high glossy blue feather, two feet in length, of the blue crane. Hanging over his shoulders and chest was a fringe three inches long of manufactured 'tails' of spotted genet and blue-grey monkey fur. Descending from his hips, almost to the knees, and completely encircling the body, was a kilt of numberless similar 'tails' of the same furs. Above each elbow were bound four dressed ox-tails, concealing the arms beneath a glossy white fringe a foot in length. Similar white ox-tails, fastened beneath the knees covered the lower leg to the ankles. Carrying in his left hand an oval ceremonial ox-hide shield, four feet long and snow white in color tempered by a single black spot and in his right a polished assegai."

After a display of mass dancing, the royal cattle—herds of them, each herd being a different color—were driven past the astonished visitors. Fynn counted one of the herds and arrived at the figure 5654. The number was greeted with hoots of derision from the members of Shaka's court. They asserted that numbers had no meaning and that Shaka's wealth was beyond computation.

While the parade of cattle was certainly impressive, as it was meant to be, something even more ominously impressive also took place. As Fynn wrote, "It became known to us that Shaka had ordered that a man standing near should be put to death, for what crime we could not learn: But we soon found it to be one of the common occurrences in the course of the day."

Fynn described the executions he witnessed during this visit: "On the first day of our visit we had seen no less than ten men carried off to death. On a mere sign by Shaka, vis: the pointing of his finger, the victim would be seized by his nearest neighbors: his neck would be twisted, and his head and body beaten with sticks, the knobs of some of these being as large as a man's fist. On each succeeding day too, numbers of others were killed: their bodies would then be carried to an adjoining hill and there impaled. We visited this spot on the fourth day. It was truly a Golgotha, swarming with hundreds of vultures."

Shaka would occasionally refer to the vultures as "The King's Birds," terrifying people with the observation that "The King's Birds" were hungry and needed to be fed.

Before retiring that first night the white men arranged a little demonstration of their own, firing their muskets into the air and shooting off a few rockets that they had brought along for just such a purpose. They were quite pleased with the excitement the noise and fire caused.

The next morning the white men were asked to attend one of the regular rituals at Bulawayo, Shaka's public bath. While he was being soaped, greased, and oiled at the riverside, Shaka would converse with his *indunas* and guests, pass judgment on cases, and order a few executions. All this took place before a large and admiring throng.

For two weeks the party of white men remained in almost constant attendance on Shaka. He displayed a keen interest in everything about European life and ways. However, in public he always made unfavorable comparisons between what he was told about Europe and the Zulu way of life. When Fynn told Shaka that Europeans used oxhide to make shoes, "He exclaimed that this was another proof of the unkindness of our forefathers, who had obliged us to protect our feet with hides for which there was no necessity—whilst he had shown the natives that the hide should be used as a more handsome and serviceable article, a shield."

Shaka's ridicule of the European way of life was greeted by loud acclamations of approval from the other Zulus. The white men, unaccustomed to being treated as inferiors by blacks, were becoming annoyed.

Fynn wrote: "Then he [Shaka] changed the conversation to the superiority of their arms, which, he said, were in many ways more advantageous than our muskets. The shield, he argued, if dipped into water previous to an attack, would be sufficient to prevent the effect of a ball fired whilst they were at a distance, and in the interval of loading they would come up to us at close quarters; we, having no shields, would then drop our guns and attempt to run; and as we could not run as fast as his soldiers, we must inevitably fall into their hands. I found it impossible to confute his arguments, as I had no acquaintance with the language, and his interpreter, on whom I had to depend, would not have dared to use strong arguments in opposition to the King. I was obliged, therefore, to accept all his decisions. . . . He placed the worst construction on everything, and did this in the presence of his subjects, ridiculing all our manners and customs, though he did this in perfect good humor."

In private Shaka indulged in less ridicule. He expressed a brotherly interest in King George of England, whom he considered a great monarch among the whites, as he, Shaka, was among the blacks. He nodded with approval when he was told that King George had only one wife and asserted that was the reason the king had been able to reach such an advanced age. But he added that it would have been wiser if King George had followed his own custom, taking no wife at all.

The gift of a small magnifying glass or burning glass intrigued the Zulu monarch. He grabbed one of his servants by the arm and held the glass over him until the focused rays of the sun had burned a small hole in the man's flesh. Though the poor fellow writhed in pain, he never made a sound. When the ordeal was over, the servant went about showing the burn to other members of the court, as though it were a badge of honor.

After two weeks, most of the white men departed for Port Natal. Shaka requested that Fynn and the Hottentot Michael stay on. A few nights later, Fynn was watching one of the seemingly endless dances that went on at the royal kraal. Suddenly a great commotion arose, and from the shouting Fynn gathered that Shaka, who had been leading the dancers, had been stabbed by an unknown attacker. Fynn found Jakot, but the interpreter was an epileptic, and the excitement had thrown him into a fit. Having picked up a rudimentary knowledge of the Zulu language during his short stay, Fynn asked those around where Shaka was, but he could get no information. People pulled him first one way and then the other. The excitement had grown so great that Fynn began to fear for his own safety. A couple of men carrying torches began to drag Fynn off, and not knowing what else to do, he agreed to follow them. They led him directly to

Shaka, who was lying severely wounded in one of the huts.

"He [Shaka] had been stabbed with an assegai through the left arm, and the blade had passed through the ribs under the left breast. It must have been due to mere accident that the wound had not penetrated the lungs, but it made the King spit blood. His own doctor, who appeared to have a good knowledge of wounds, gave him a vomit, and afterwards repeated doses of purging medicine, and continually washed the wound with concoctions of cooling roots. He also probed the wound to ascertain whether any poison had been used on the assegai."

Fynn had originally been trained as a surgeon's assistant and put his own medical knowledge to work in washing and dressing Shaka's wound. But Shaka apparently believed that he was going to die. "He declaimed nearly the whole night, expecting that only fateful consequences would ensue."

The crowds that pressed in around Shaka's hut were becoming more and more hysterical. Fynn wrote: "Morning showed a horrid sight in a clear light. I am satisfied that I cannot describe the scene in any words that would be of force to convey an impression to any reader sufficiently distinct of that hideous scene. Immense crowds of people were constantly arriving and began their shouts when they came in sight of the kraal, running and exerting their utmost powers of voice as they entered it. They joined those already there, pulling one another about, throwing themselves down, without heeding how they fell, men and women indiscriminately. Many fainted from over-exertion and excessive heat. . . . They had begun to kill one another. Some were put to death because they did not weep, others for putting spittle in their eyes, others for sitting down to cry, although strength and tears, after such continuous exertion and mourning, were wholly exhausted."

Eventually the Zulus began to piece together the story of the assassination attempt. There had been several assassins, and six other men were wounded at the same time that Shaka was stabbed. The assassins had escaped, but from the direction they took it was assumed that they had been sent by Shaka's old enemy Zwide and were attempting to return to him. The actual origin of this attempt on Shaka's life has never been determined. It appears, however, that Zwide had died at about the same time, and the assassination may have been part of the *ihlambo* (the washing of the spears in blood), a ceremonial cleansing that concluded a period of mourning. It seems likely, therefore, that the man behind the attempt was Zwide's son and heir, Sikhunyana.

Zulu search parties found three men who may, or may not, have been the assassins. They killed all three and dragged their bodies back to a spot about a mile from the royal kraal. The multitude from the kraal began streaming past the bodies, and as each person passed he struck the corpses with a stick that was then dropped on the spot. Soon the bodies were completely covered, and nothing could be seen but an immense pile of sticks.

The ears had been cut from the three victims, and these were ceremonially burned. Shaka had regained enough strength by this time to attend the burning. As he began to recover, order was gradually restored. Fynn observed: "From the moment that Shaka had been stabbed, there had been a prohibition to wear ornaments, to wash the body or to shave; and no man whose wife was pregnant had been allowed to come into the King's presence. All transgressions of these regulations being punishable with death, several human beings had been put to death. . . . The restoration of the King's health made some great changes. The tumult gradually ceased."

A force was dispatched to the former Ndwandwe country. The troops were ordered to spare no one, and when they returned a few days later, bringing eight hundred head of captured cattle with them, Shaka was pleased. His recovery from what he had believed was a fatal wound had put him in an excellent mood.

At that moment Farewell arrived back at Bulawayo, bearing a long and imposing-looking document that he wished Shaka to sign. Though the phraseology was vague, deliberately confusing, and often downright incomprehensible, the document amounted to a deed giving Farewell and his associates absolute title to Port Natal and some thirty-five hundred square miles of surrounding territory.

A formal signing ceremony was held, which Shaka seemed to enjoy hugely. Farewell and his associates signed the deed, while Shaka and several of his *indunas* put their marks on it. Shaka clearly had no idea what the document said, or what signing it meant. In fact, it meant nothing at all. Later he cheerfully signed similar documents for other white traders. Shaka had no intention of giving away any land under his control. At most he was willing to grant the white settlers the right to establish small colonies and to maintain a certain degree of self-government, just as if they had been powerful local chiefs. For the rest, he was merely humoring his interesting and perhaps useful visitors.

Shaka and Farewell parted on friendly terms, each apparently sure that he had outsmarted the other.

VII

The Zulu Empire

In the years between the Second Ndwandwe War in 1820 and the visit of the white traders in 1824, a great deal had happened in Zululand. Zwide's defeat and the flight of the Ndwandwe survivors marked a turning point in Shaka's career and in the history of Africa.

The chain of migrations and wars associated with the expansion of Shaka's empire has been called *Mfecane,* a Nguni word which means "The Crushing." The force of the *Mfecane* radiated in all directions from the Zulu state.

In 1820 Shaka's *impis* conducted raids across the Buffalo River, which had for a short time served as the western boundary of Zulu expansion. Two large tribes, the Tembu and Cunu, tried to block the Zulu advance. The Tembu were defeated and their cattle taken to feed the Zulu *impis*. The Cunu, however, managed to administer a sharp though temporary setback to the Zulus. Knowing that there would be no safety within reach of Shaka's *impis,* both tribes left their homelands and fled southward beyond the Tugela River. Southern Natal was already filling up with refugees from Shaka's wars, and the Tembu, bereft of their cattle, tried to make up the loss by raiding the herds of others. And so it went.

To make matters worse, the Zulu *impis* were already beginning to raid south of the Tugela, further disrupting the life of the tribes living in this region and pressing them harder upon one another.

For two seasons, however, the Zulu armies stayed relatively near home. They were engaged in exterminating the last holdouts to Shaka's rule in Zululand proper, "sweeping up the rubbish," as Shaka called this activity. Shaka's energies were also engaged in resettling the former Ndwandwe area, which had been virtually depopulated by the Zulus.

In 1822, the Zulu armies were again on the march southward over the Tugela River. They scattered the dispirited tribes in the region and drove the survivors either across the Drakensburg Range or farther south. This southward pressure was ultimately felt by the Xhosa clans living on the frontier between the Bantu and the Europeans at the southern tip of Africa.

In the years between 1822 and 1824 continual Zulu raids created a virtually uninhabited strip one hundred miles wide, south of the Tugela River. Only handfuls of half-starved refugees too terrified to plant crops or keep cattle managed to eke out an existence in this region. Cannibalism flourished, and the refugees were continually pursued by Zulu *impis,* who regularly patrolled the region.

It was not mere savagery but military strategy that led Shaka to depopulate this large area. The existence of the wasteland (what would be called a traffic desert in modern military terms) made escape to the south from Shaka's kingdom virtually impossible. An invasion of Zululand through this "desert" would be even more difficult, since the land could provide no food for an army.

During this period Shaka committed one of his very few military errors. He allowed his favorite, Mzilikazi, to again assume the chieftaincy of the Kumalo clan. For a time Mzilikazi seemed content to remain a loyal vassal. Acting on Shaka's orders, Mzilikazi and his Kumalo warriors raided northward. The raids were enormously successful, and unexpectedly large numbers of cattle were seized. Shaka assumed that the bulk of the cattle would be sent directly to him, but the haul was so great that Mzilikazi assumed Shaka would never know that the Kumalo had retained much more than their usual percentage. Mzilikazi had reckoned without Shaka's efficient spy system. When the Zulu ruler learned of the holding back of cattle, he sent messengers to Mzilikazi demanding that all the beasts be accounted for. Mzilikazi, strongly supported by the members of his clan, decided to resist Shaka's orders. In a gesture of defiance, he cut the ostrich feather plumes from the messengers' headdresses and sent them back to Shaka with an impudent reply.

Mzilikazi and his clan then retired to their mountain stronghold and prepared for the inevitable Zulu attack. When the attack came it was uncharacteristically half-hearted, and the Zulus were easily repulsed. Strangely, Shaka did not seem particularly upset by the loss and did not order the execution of the "cowards" who had failed to defeat Mzilikazi. Stranger still, Shaka seemed content to let the matter rest there. However, his military *indunas* insisted that such an open affront to Zulu power could not be allowed to go unpunished. Finally, Shaka was forced to launch a second and more vigorous attack.

The Zulus found a Kumalo deserter who was able to lead them directly into Mzilikazi's stronghold, and the Kumalo were overrun in a bloody engagement. But again the Zulus seemed to act with unusual restraint. Mzilikazi and several hundred of his followers were permitted to escape, joining the ever-growing number of refugees from Zulu power.

Perhaps Shaka allowed his admiration for Mzilikazi's military skills and his gratitude to the Kumalo clan to temper his usual harshness. We will never know for certain.

In subsequent years, Mzilikazi was to become, next to Shaka, the most successful of the Nguni conquerors. He imitated Shaka's methods closely and they worked well for him, as they had for Shaka.

After being exposed to Zulu attacks for several years, most of the Nguni tribes adopted the stabbing assegai and many of the other Zulu fighting methods. The Zulus could no longer depend upon surprise to give them victory, yet their forces had become virtually irresistible. Europeans who traveled frequently in Zululand during the later days of Shaka's rule noted that the Zulu warriors were in no way stronger or braver than the warriors they consistently defeated. What, then, accounted for Zulu superiority? The secret seems to lie primarily in the incredible Zulu discipline, an efficient espionage system, and the reputation for invincibility that the names "Zulu" or "Shaka" inspired throughout southern Africa.

The Zulu warrior knew that he faced death from two sources. If he fought well, he would expose himself to death in battle. But if he held back and attempted to preserve his life during a battle, he would almost surely be executed as a coward. After each battle Shaka, accompanied by a retinue of his slayers, would walk through the ranks and ask each of the commanders to point out "the cowards." These men would be clubbed to death immediately. It was far more dangerous to attempt to avoid death on the battlefield than to place oneself in the front ranks. Even the suspicion of cowardice would bring death. Each Zulu fought as hard as possible, so that there could be no question of his bravery. However, many brave warriors were executed anyway, for if the commanders did not point out a certain number of men to be killed, Shaka would accuse them of shielding cowards.

For all his apparent indifference to the fate of his soldiers, Shaka was careful not to risk their lives needlessly. Though there was much talk of war, Shaka preferred to avoid a pitched battle and to defeat an enemy by trickery, as in the case of the secret attack on the Ndwandwe in the forest, or to overwhelm them with the sheer terror inspired by the reputation of the Zulu *impis*. Often the knowledge that any resistance would result in complete annihilation was enough to make an enemy offer submission without a fight.

But in order to maintain their reputation for invincibility, the Zulus were sometimes forced to undertake unprofitable and dangerous attacks. One such attack was directed against the mountain stronghold of the Pepeta clan. The Pepeta were a small and impoverished people. They presented no danger to the Zulus, and they had nothing worth taking. Shaka could easily have ignored them, but since they represented a point of resistance, they had to be crushed.

Ordinary Zulu battlefield techniques would not work against the strongly entrenched mountain clan. The attackers had to pass through a valley. On the heights above were the Pepetas—men, women, and children—all throwing down rocks and spears with devastating accuracy. In order to survive this barrage, Shaka instructed a column of his warriors to put their shields over their heads in such a way that they overlapped with one another and formed a protective roof. The Romans had often employed the same sort of "tortoise" formation; the Zulus called the formation *Isongololo Lika Shaka* (Shaka's millipede).

Shaka's troops were able to penetrate the stronghold, though they suffered considerable losses in the process. Rather than face the inevitable massacre, many of the Pepetas threw themselves from the heights. This led to the spreading of a legend that one of Shaka's favorite methods of execution was to march his victims off the side of a cliff.

Says Shaka's biographer, E. A. Ritter, "Here lies the origin of the fantastic tales one hears about nearly every precipice and waterfall in Zululand and the greater part of Natal and Pondoland." It was often reported that Shaka even used this method of execution at his royal kraals. But Ritter points out, "A study of the topography surrounding these old sites will reveal that the execution parties, and the supposedly gloating Shaka would have been compelled to march from fifteen to twenty-five miles to find any cliff or waterfall which could have been used for such a purpose."

The terror Shaka inspired among his own subjects was as great if not greater than that which he inspired among his enemies. To a certain extent all Bantu chiefs and headmen wore the mantle of supernatural powers. There were religious rituals that only the chief could perform, and he was regarded as something of a god. Even a petty chief was treated with elaborate deference by his subjects. The common people were not allowed to stand or speak in a chief's presence unless asked to do so. In Shaka's case, these elaborate courtesies were no mere formalities. Any breach of court etiquette, merely sneezing or belching in the king's presence, could bring a death sentence to any but the most favored of his subjects. Such a breach detracted from the royal dignity, and it was vital to Shaka that his very presence radiate a sense of overpowering and irresistible force.

Many have come to believe that Shaka was so powerful that there were no forces within the Zulu state that had any effect on his actions. This is what

Shaka wanted his subjects to think, but it was not true.

Shaka had created a huge army, the mere existence of which exerted tremendous pressure on the chief. The army was continually hungry for both beef and glory. Soldiers did not plant crops or keep cattle and so could not create any wealth for the state. They were able to feed themselves only by plundering others. The herds and fields of Zululand could not produce enough to feed this huge mass of hungry men, nor were there any occupations beside warfare that seemed worthwhile to the young warriors. Shaka might kill an individual soldier or even an *induna,* but he could not afford to offend the army as a whole. He was, therefore, forced to pursue a policy of continual warfare. Even if he had wished to cease the raids on neighboring tribes (and there is no indication that he did), he could not have. In the case of the attack on Mzilikazi, it appears that Shaka was compelled by his *indunas* to make war even though he was not enthusiastic about it. In this way the military *indunas* had replaced the elders as the chief pressure on the king.

Even "public opinion" had to be taken into account. When Shaka wished to institute a policy he believed would be widely unpopular he often had the "suggestion" presented by a powerful *induna.* Shaka would then appear to agree reluctantly to this "suggestion" because it was a necessity. By such means he sought to remove from his own shoulders the burden of unpopular policies, while at the same time he tried to portray himself as a monarch who could do as he wished.

Shaka also retained an old custom that tempered the image of omnipotence he had created. During one of the principal harvest ceremonies the people were allowed to speak freely in front of the king. They could ask him anything, and he was required to answer honestly. No one was to suffer for having asked an embarrassing or difficult question. Whether, in practice, people really spoke freely in front of Shaka is doubtful. But it is significant that Shaka never felt strong enough to abolish the practice.

Most of the time Shaka was treated as an all-powerful god. In public he was preceded by two *imbongi* or official praise singers. It was the job of the praise singers loudly to proclaim the greatness of Shaka's deeds and to repeat his praise names *No-dumeglezi* (Sitting Thunder) and *Sigidi* (One Thousand, or He Who Is Equal to One Thousand). Shaka's own name was too awesome even to be spoken by ordinary people. They usually called him "The Great Elephant."

As chief judge as well as king, Shaka spent a good deal of time sitting in judgment on cases that did not directly concern royal affairs. His decision in all cases was final. The single word *"Ngitshila"* ("I have spoken") was enough to end any argument.

Shaka's pronouncements were greeted by the Zulus with the royal salute *"Bayete!"* ("Hail!") or by loud shouts of *"Yebo"* ("Yes") or *"Yebo, Baba"* ("Yes, Father"). Even those condemned to death often marched off shouting the praises of the king who had just condemned them. They had no hope that by this display of loyalty their sentences would be altered, for Shaka never changed his mind. It was rather that they held Shaka in such awe that even their own condemnations were looked upon as acts of greatness.

Shaka's methods of breaking down the traditional ties of kinship so that all loyalty would be centered on the king could be extremely cruel. People were not allowed to shed tears for the death of anyone except a member of the royal family. Occasionally Shaka would even order a father to kill his own son. If there was a moment's hesitation, he might order both father and son and perhaps the entire family to be slain.

One of the white men who was an observer at Shaka's court wrote: "Thus a father did not hesitate to be the executioner of his own child; the ties of consanguinity availed nothing with the tyrant, his decrees must be carried into operation, and that unhesitatingly; and if after perpetrating the revolting deed the feelings of nature should predominate, and manifest themselves to the inhuman savage, the party was instantly ordered to be despatched with the atrocious remark, 'Take the *umtakati* away; let me see if loving his child better than his King will do him any good. See if your clubs are not harder than his head.'"

During this period Shaka continued his struggle against the *isangomas* or witch doctors, most tenacious and dangerous of his internal enemies. He finally managed to break their power thoroughly by means of a cunning trick. One evening when the guards around his hut had been sent to another part of the

royal kraal, Shaka spattered the outside of the hut
with animal blood. Only Shaka and a trusted servant
knew who had done this.

When the sun rose the next morning and the people saw what had happened, they were horrified. To
stain the king's hut with blood was evidence of the
most dire witchcraft. When Shaka came out of his
hut to see what the commotion was about, he, too,
professed horror. "Blood calls for blood," he thun-
dered. He decreed that in seven days the entire adult
male population of Zululand would gather at Bulawayo and there would be a great "smelling out."

On the appointed day all the witch finders in the
land were split up into teams, so that they could work
more quickly in "smelling out" the huge crowd. Contrary to usual practice, however, those accused were
not dragged off and killed at once. They were all placed
together, for Shaka had ordered that when the "smelling out" was completed there would be a mass execution of the *umtakati*.

The witch finders went at their work with great
relish, sensing an opportunity to regain some of their
lost power. They accused many of Shaka's most
trusted associates, including the servant who had been
in on the scheme. These men, some angry, others
simply frightened, sat for hours expecting that by the
time the sun went down that night they would be
dead.

Only one of the *isangoma* refused to accuse anyone.
When Shaka asked him who had committed the deed,
the man said it was *izulu*. Most listeners were shocked
by the statement, but Shaka himself was enormously

pleased. *Izulu* was a word with a double meaning. It could mean "heaven" or it could be used as a praise name for the king. Shaka, who was himself a great punster, appreciated the man's acuteness in discerning the trap. He also enjoyed the clever way the *isangoma* had made clear that he knew what was happening. In the end virtually all of the *isangoma,* with the exception of the punster, were executed by their would-be victims.

Later Mzilikazi, who imitated Shaka in most things, used virtually the same trick against the witch doctors among his own followers. He put a stone in his mouth and ordered the *isangomas* to "smell out" the person who had caused the swelling. When the *isangomas* picked out several people, Mzilikazi spat out the stone and had the *isangomas* executed.

The destruction of the power of the witch doctors among the Zulus did not mean the end of all executions for witchcraft. Shaka himself now became the primary *isangoma.* According to some accounts he declared that he was the only witch finder in the country, for if he had rivals his life would be insecure.

As the chief controller of magic, Shaka had concentrated enormous power in his own hands. The intense fear that had been felt toward the *isangomas* was now directed toward the monarch. His commands, like those of a god, could neither be questioned nor understood. They merely had to be obeyed. Moreover, the feeling grew among Shaka's subjects that the king knew all their innermost thoughts.

VIII

The Destroyer

ACCORDING TO LEGEND, Alexander the Great once wept at the thought that he had no more worlds left to conquer. There were times when Shaka seems to have been moved by similar feelings. One of the Zulu chants composed in his honor went:

> Thou hast finished off the tribes
> Where wilt thou wage war?
> Yes! where wilt thou wage war?
> Thou hast conquered the Kings
> Where wilt thou wage war?
> Thou hast finished off the tribes
> Where wilt thou wage war?
> Yes! yes! yes! where wilt thou wage war?

This was an exaggeration, of course. There were plenty of unconquered tribes in southern Africa. But Shaka's empire was beginning to reach its natural limits. There was only so far that even the battle-hardened Zulu *impis* could travel. To the north of the Pongola River the land was inhospitable and unfamiliar. This was malaria country, and the Zulus, accustomed to the healthy climate of their own homeland, quickly sickened and died there. To the west there were mountains and jungles in which the Zulu armies could not operate efficiently. To the south, Shaka's conquests had extended so far that he was in danger of coming into conflict with the Europeans pushing up from the Cape Colony.

The Zulu king now faced a new problem. He had a huge army sitting around with little to do. Shaka complained bitterly that the army was "eating him up," which was almost true. Since the troops were fed at the king's expense they were a severe drain on his resources, and when they were not fighting, they were not bringing anything in.

Idle warriors were also potentially dangerous. Discipline tended to break down in peacetime. Rivalries and intrigues developed quickly among men who had nothing to do. Occasionally Shaka would schedule inspection trips to the various military kraals in his domain just to keep his men active. When these trips were led by the king himself, they could be as taxing and dangerous for the soldiers as a long military campaign. Shaka was accustomed to travel fifty miles a day at a fast trot. Anyone who lagged behind or in any other way displeased the king was immediately stabbed by Shaka's ever-present slayers. Fynn, who witnessed one of these marches, described a typical scene:

"When he, Shaka, perceived that the regiment was not yet moving he ordered his servants to run and stab a few of them. They did so and killed five. The regiment then ran on ahead with all possible speed to lead the way and clear it of thorns, the omission to do which, in accordance with the usual practice, they supposed was the reason why the servants were killing them. In their haste a group of men passed within five yards of Shaka, not having noticed him until they got within that distance. He looked at them so fiercely as to make them run back, whereupon he vociferated his usual oath . . . then ordered an attendant to single out a man and stab him. They sat down, about 80 in number, when the attendant for some moments looked about for a bad looking man; he found one, then stabbed him in the left breast and, by Shaka's orders, left the assegai in the body that it might be seen by passers-by. The moment the assegai pierced the body Shaka averted his head, his countenance betraying something like a feeling of horror, but we had not proceeded more than a mile when two other unfortunates experienced the same fate."

In 1825 one of the most important of the early white pioneers arrived in Natal. He was seventeen-year-old Nathaniel Isaacs, son of a fairly prominent Anglo-Jewish family. Isaacs had been sent to work for an uncle on the island of St. Helena. He arrived there shortly after the island's most famous prisoner, Napoleon Bonaparte, died. Young Isaacs found St. Helena almost as much of a prison as Napoleon had. Life in his uncle's counting house did not suit him. When the chance arose to join the Farewell Trading

Company's expedition in Natal, young Isaacs jumped at it.

Isaacs was to become one of Shaka's closest white associates. His importance lies in the fact that he was an enthusiastic diarist who recorded everything he saw or experienced in the land of the Zulus. Isaacs was not a trained observer, nor was he particularly well educated. He misnamed practically every plant and animal he encountered. His attempts to translate the Zulu language are among the worst on record. He overwrote shamefully and had a strong tendency to dramatize events and the part he played in them. Yet with all these reservations, Nathaniel Isaacs' writings contain the most complete and accurate account of the Zulu empire as it was under Shaka.

Henry Fynn also wrote about Shaka, but the account he wrote while Shaka was still alive was lost. Many years later Fynn tried to reconstruct events from rough notes and memory. Fynn was a more objective observer, but memory tends to blunt events. Isaacs' first-hand account provides a truer picture.

Shaka's army did not remain idle for long. In 1826 his most persistent enemies, the Ndwandwes, presented another challenge. Zwide was dead, and one of his sons, Sikhunyana, had succeeded him. This succession was contested by another son, Sompaunga, who was defeated in 1826. Sompaunga fled to Shaka's protection, bringing with him valuable information concerning Ndwandwe plans. Shaka was delighted with the prospect of war and quickly mobilized an army of forty thousand to meet the new Ndwandwe threat. Serving in the army was an "English Musket Corps" consisting of Fynn, Farewell, and some of the other settlers from Port Natal who had agreed to help Shaka in order to retain the king's good will. Also included was the interpreter Jakot.

Shaka's force crossed the Pongola River, which was considered the northern boundary of the Zulu empire, and met the Ndwandwes at a hilly spot about twenty miles east of the present town of Utrecht. The battle started when Jakot fired three shots from his ancient musket into the Ndwandwe ranks. Other than that the "Musket Corps" played no significant part in the contest.

The Ndwandwe army was approximately the same size as that of the Zulus, and by this time the Ndwandwes had thoroughly mastered the stabbing assegai and other Zulu fighting techniques. Both sides charged. For some moments there was bloody hand-to-hand combat. When the two armies fell back to assess their losses it was clear that the Zulus had gotten the better of the clash, though their losses had also been heavy. In a succeeding engagement the Ndwandwes weakened visibly. A third Zulu charge broke them entirely, and a terrible massacre followed. As a result of this battle the Ndwandwes, who had been one of the largest and most powerful of the Nguni tribes, were virtually eliminated as an independent force. The survivors made their way to the camps of others who had already fled from the Zulus.

Shaka's hatred of the Ndwandwes provides a striking contrast with his apparent admiration for the small but troublesome Kumalo clan—the clan from which the rebel Mzilikazi had come. The Kumalo stoutly resisted incorporation into the Zulu empire, and two Kumalo chiefs, Beje and Mlotsha, were accused of aiding the Ndwandwes. Shaka decided that the time had come to deal with these chiefs. Unaccountably he sent a young and inexperienced regiment against Beje and his people who lived near the Ngome Forest, a terrain made difficult by thick vegetation and mountains. Beje's soldiers had become experts at conducting guerrilla warfare against the Zulus. So famous was their resistance that "Beje is in the Ngome" is still a Zulu proverb. Beje administered a sharp setback to the inexperienced Zulu invaders, but Shaka did not execute any of the defeated warriors as "cowards."

Still, something had to be done about the troublesome chieftain. Unexpectedly, Shaka was presented with an opportunity to use his "Musket Corps" against the Kumalo. Michael and John, two of the Englishmen's Hottentot servants, had gotten drunk and raped the young wife of a Zulu chief. Shaka, who didn't like Hottentots anyway, loudly threatened to wipe out the entire Port Natal settlement. Isaacs did not believe that Shaka was as angry as he appeared to be, but he feared that one of the *indunas* would take the king's words seriously and actually launch such an attack.

Isaacs' appraisal proved correct. In private the Zulu king told the whites that he had to do something about the rape, or the *indunas* would think he was no longer fit to lead. What he had decided to do was to send a group of Port Natal settlers, armed with muskets, to take part in an attack on Beje. In all probability, Shaka had not feared his *indunas* at all but was simply looking for an excuse to involve the Port Natal settlers and their muskets in the difficult attack. As usual, he blamed the decision on someone else.

Fynn and Farewell begged off the expedition, so Isaacs was chosen to lead the Musket Corps, which was made up of Jakot and ten other armed men. They were backed by an entire regiment of Zulus. Shaka had publicly ordered the extermination of the Kumalo, but judging by the way the Zulu regiment behaved, it seems likely that they had been given very different orders in private. The campaign was really rather ridiculous. About fifty of the Kumalo and their cattle were spotted at the edge of the forest. Isaacs led his little party forward and fired a volley at them.

"The report of our muskets reverberated from the rocks, and struck terror into the enemy; they shouted and ran in all directions, and the Zulus some considerable distance behind us, were observed all lying on the ground with their faces under, and their shields on their backs. This singular maneuver of the Zulus had a terrible effect on the enemy, who seeing the others [Zulus] fall at the report of the musketry, concluded they were all dead and ran off to avoid coming into contact with us."

There were several other desultory skirmishes. During one of them Isaacs was wounded in the back by a spear and had a harrowing experience with a Zulu witch doctor, who tried to cure the wound by making him drink various potions, which Isaacs found worse than the wound itself.

At this point envoys from the Kumalo appeared and offered to surrender. They brought with them some half-starved cattle and goats as tribute. One of the Port Natal sailors suggested that ten women be added to the tribute, "by way of cementing friendship by nuptial ties." The Kumalo agreed, and Beje was once again left in peace.

Shaka seemed satisfied with this meager victory. He gave Isaacs a few cows and granted him the praise name Dambuza, which Isaacs freely translated as "The Brave Warrior Who Was Wounded at Ngome." But he also told Isaacs that he would have executed any Zulu who had dared to return from battle with a wound in the back.

The other Kumalo chief, Mlotsha, fared less well. He retreated to his mountain fortress but found that it was poorly provisioned. The Zulus besieged him, forcing him to surrender. But here, too, Shaka was surprisingly lenient. He spared Mlotsha, and according to Zulu legends, even sent the chief a personal message to ease the humiliation of defeat. Mlotsha was a celebrated rainmaker, and Shaka told him that he was the greatest rain chief, "And I am the greatest war chief. Let each stick to his own business. . . ."

A foreshadowing of future trouble for the Zulu *impis* could be found in the disaster that befell a cattle-raiding expedition that Shaka sent early in 1827 against some small tribes to the north of the Zulu lands. The northerners retreated, leading the Zulus deeper into the unfamiliar and disease-ridden country. A third of the entire Zulu force became infected with malaria or dysentery and was too weak to fight or even to march. The commander split his force into two groups, leaving the badly weakened men to rest and taking the healthiest on a search for cattle and other provisions.

The cattle-hunting Zulus ran afoul of a large party of Griquas, descendants of Europeans and Hottentots. The Griquas had become a sort of third force in southern Africa. They were not numerous, but they had horses and firearms, and this made them formidable enemies. For a time they were even able to establish a small Griqua republic.

Shaka had often discussed with his commanders how Zulus could overcome firearms. Mdlaka, leader of the Zulus, attempted to put some of Shaka's ideas into use in this encounter, but the Griquas would not cooperate. The Zulus charged; the Griquas fired. Then, instead of standing and reloading so that the Zulus could overrun them, the Griquas rode back out of range, reloaded, charged, and fired again. After a few volleys, the Zulus realized that they were going to be cut to pieces in this sort of warfare. They retreated to a hilly region, the sort of land where Shaka believed the advantage of horses would be reduced. According to Shaka's theory, the more numerous Zulus could then overcome armed and mounted men. The Griquas saw the danger, broke off the battle, and simply rode away, leaving the Zulus puzzled and frustrated.

Meanwhile, those Zulus who had been too sick to march were attacked by local tribesmen and badly mauled. So, having sustained heavy losses and having captured only a handful of cattle, the raiding army returned home to face Shaka's anger.

Shaka could not understand how the lightly regarded northern tribes had been able to do so much damage to his troops. He had no experience with the dangers of disease and assumed that the weakened troops had simply not taken adequate care of their food supply. Such negligence was considered a breach of discipline, and Shaka ordered the execution of an entire regiment of the raiders as punishment.

Personal troubles also began to assail Shaka. In 1821 his grandmother, Mtaniya, died. She was a very old woman and had been ill for some time. Shaka asked Fynn, the former surgeon's assistant, to attend her.

"I accordingly went to see her. As her age was about eighty, I saw no hope of recovery, and candidly told the King my fears. He requested me to put a white shirt on her. I did so. He then began to cry bitterly. Jacob [Jakot] the interpreter, told me of Shaka's great affection for his grandmother. When she happened to visit him he frequently washed her eyes and ears, which were in a sad state because of her age; he also pared her nails and otherwise treated her as a father might his child. We could hardly believe that a man of an apparent unfeeling disposition could be possessed of such affection and consideration for others. Further observation, however, convinced us that this was indeed the case."

When the old woman died Shaka ordered a general mourning. Several persons were executed for not showing sufficient grief. It was only a hint of what was to come.

Shaka was turning increasingly brooding and angry. Late in 1826 he dreamed that some of the boys in the kraal had been sneaking into his personal harem at night. As a matter of fact they probably had been. Shaka kept an enormous number of young women locked up in his seraglios, and they chafed under the restrictions. Many kings had used eunuchs to guard their harems, but this practice was unknown among the Zulus, who would probably have regarded such mutilation as unnaturally cruel. For harem guards, Shaka simply picked the ugliest men he could find, but the system did not work very well. There was a good deal of nightly traffic over the seraglio walls, and even Isaacs seems to have engaged in it. Shaka probably turned a blind eye to what was going on, until his dream. After that, however, he gathered a group of warriors and announced he was going on a long trip. He then marched a few miles from the kraal, told his companions about the dream, and asked them what he should do with the boys who had violated his harem. Their response was, "Father, kill them, for they are not fit to live."

Marching back to the kraal, he ordered his men to surround it. Isaacs' account tells what happened next: "He then ordered the victims intended for destruction to be brought to him, and those whom he selected were immediately despatched. He began by taking out several fine lads and ordering their own brothers to twist their necks, their bodies were afterwards dragged away and beaten with sticks until life was extinct.

After this refined act of monstrous cruelty, the remainder of the victims in the kraal were indiscriminately butchered. Few of the poor innocent children cried or evinced any sorrow. . . ." One hundred and seventy were killed in all.

Isaacs also recorded that he had seen Shaka beating his own mother, Nandi, because "she had not taken proper care of his girls." Isaacs had become used to the frequent executions at Bulawayo, but this "slaughter of the innocents," as he termed it, seemed to be something different, and for the first time Shaka really began to frighten him. He was relieved when his stay at the Zulu king's kraal ended.

After his grandmother's death, Shaka began to worry increasingly about his own age. He was approaching forty, and the first flecks of gray had begun to appear in his hair. Considering that he had once derided, and then executed the old men, his own advancing age had ominous overtones.

Sometime during the course of his conversations with the white men one of them had mentioned a preparation called Rowland's Macassar Oil. It was England's leading hair dressing and was supposed to stop falling hair and restore hair to its original color. Actually, it did neither, being merely olive oil with some sweet-smelling substance added. But Shaka somehow got the idea that the oil was a sort of rejuvenating preparation that would make he and Nandi, who was now beginning to slow down with age, look and feel younger once again. Perhaps the Englishmen encouraged this misconception, or perhaps the obsession was the result of Shaka's own fears of growing old. He continually pestered the Englishmen for a bottle of the hair oil, but in Natal it was not easy to come by.

Shaka now spent a great deal of time with the visiting Englishmen and seemed to enjoy their company. However, his true feelings toward whites are difficult to determine. He named one of his female regiments the *Ngisimane,* which means "the Englishmen," but there is a question as to whether this was meant as a sincere compliment or whether it was intended as an ironic comment on the fighting ability of the white men.

In July 1827 Shaka conceived the idea of sending a diplomatic mission to King George. Among the things he hoped to accomplish was to secure a bottle of Rowland's Macassar Oil from the English king. To head the mission he picked a British naval officer named King, who was at Port Natal. Lieutenant King was to be accompanied by several Zulu *indunas.*

Plans for the mission were temporarily suspended when Shaka received the news that Nandi was gravely ill. The king, who had been hunting, immediately broke off the hunt to return home. Nandi was in a coma when Shaka arrived. He asked Fynn to examine her, but Fynn's diagnosis contained no good news. "Her complaint was dysentery; and I reported at once to Shaka that her case was hopeless and that I did not expect that she would live through the day."

Shaka sat down, head bowed, and did not say a word for several hours. When he was brought the news that Nandi was dead, he rose and went to his own special hut. A short time later he emerged in full war regalia. He then went to Nandi's hut, followed by his principal *indunas,* also in their war attire, what happened next was related by Fynn.

"For about twenty minutes," wrote Fynn, "he stood in a silent mournful attitude with his head bowed upon his shield, on which I saw large tears fall, occasionally wiping them away with his right hand. He presented the appearance of a brave warrior in extreme distress, sufficient to extort pity and commiseration from the hardest of hearts. After two or three deep sighs his feelings became ungovernable, he broke out into frantic yells, which fearfully contrasted with the silence that had hitherto prevailed. The signal was enough. The chiefs and people, to the number of about fifteen thousand, commenced the most dismal and horrid lamentations. The people from the neighboring kraals, male and female, came pouring in, each body as they came in sight, at a distance of half a mile, joining to swell the terrible cry. Through the whole night it continued, none daring to rest or refresh themselves with water; while at short intervals, fresh outbursts were heard as more distant regiments approached. The morning dawned without any relaxation, and before noon the number had increased to about sixty thousand. The cries now became indescribably horrid. Hundreds were lying faint from excessive fatigue and want of nourishment; while the carcasses of forty oxen lay in a heap, which had been slaughtered as an offering to the guardian spirits of the tribe. At noon the whole force formed a circle with Shaka in the center, and sang a war song, which afforded them some relaxation during its con-

tinuance. At the close of it, Shaka ordered several
men to be executed on the spot; and the cries became
if possible, more violent than ever. No further orders
were needed; but, as if bent on convincing their chief
of their extreme grief the multitude commenced a
general massacre. Many of them received the blow of
death while inflicting it on others, each taking the
opportunity of revenging his injuries, real or imaginary. Those who could no more force tears from
their eyes—those who were found near the river
panting for water—were beaten to death by others
who were mad with excitement. Towards the after-
noon I calculated that not fewer than seven thousand
people had fallen in this frightful indiscriminate massacre. The adjacent stream, to which many had fled
exhausted to wet their parched tongues, became im-
passable from the number of dead corpses which lay
on each side of it; while the kraal in which the scene
took place, was flowing with blood."

On the third day after her death, Nandi was buried.
Ten of her servants, their arms and legs broken according to Zulu custom, were buried alive with her.
An entire regiment of twelve thousand men was ordered to guard the grave for a year. They were to be
supplied with fifteen thousand cattle taken from every
kraal in the country.

After the burial, one of Shaka's principal *indunas*
announced further conditions for the mourning period. "As The Great Female Elephant [a praise name
for the Zulu Queen Mother]—the ever ruling spirit
of Vegetation had died, and it was probable that the
heavens and the earth would unite in bewailing her

death, the sacrifice should be a great one: No cultivation should be allowed during the following year; no milk should be used, but as drawn from the cow it should be all poured upon the earth; and all women who should be found with child during the year should, with their husbands be put to death."

Some restrictions during a mourning period were traditional among the Zulus, but these were dangerously extreme. The crops had already been planted, so there was no imminent prospect of starvation, but if all the restrictions were to be carried out for a full year the Zulu nation faced ruin.

Shaka apparently had every intention of enforcing the prohibitions. He commanded his warriors to scour the land and kill everyone who did not seem to be grieving enough. He complained of dreams in which his long dead foster-father, Mbiya, had told him that Nandi had been killed by sorcery. As a result, he ordered a large number of women burned alive as *umtakati*.

Many have speculated that the impact of Nandi's death actually drove Shaka temporarily mad. But Fynn and Isaacs, who were on the scene, took a more cynical view of events. Isaacs had been away hunting when Nandi died but returned to the royal kraal shortly afterward. He wrote in his journal that the "horrible and fiendish slaughter was continued for a fortnight, to strike the people with terror, and make them approach the insatiable monster [Shaka] with awe. He had an impression also, that by a decree so ferocious and bloody the people would live in fear of his dying, when similar massacres would ensue; and that to avoid them they would do all in their power to preserve the life of their monarch."

A few days later Isaacs wrote, "The King is a dissembler and a most professed hypocrite."

Years later, Fynn, reflecting on the time of mourning for Nandi, wrote: "When Shaka shed a tear, which he often did, the howlings were renewed. This I think, he often did from political motives. After mature reflection I think I may safely assert that the whole thing was nothing more than a political scheme . . . in furtherance of Shaka's vain imaginations and to keep the minds of his people filled with wonder."

Shaka's grief, real or feigned, began to subside after three months. According to tradition, it was a man named Gala of the Biyela clan who finally had the courage to speak up to Shaka and break the hold of the excessive mourning for Nandi. Gala reminded the king that other members of the royal family had died in the past but that no such disastrous prohibitions had been introduced. He warned, "You have destroyed the country. Your country will be inhabited by other kings for your people will perish of famine." He urged Shaka to "stuff a stone into his stomach"— a Zulu expression that means buck up, or take courage—and concluded, "This is not the first time anyone has died in Zululand."

Instead of executing Gala, as he might well have done, Shaka rewarded him for speaking the harsh truth. Gala was given a supply of cattle and allowed to assume the headring, a permission granted only to those who had distinguished themselves by extreme bravery.

IX

Assassination

Sincere or not, Shaka used his grief over Nandi's death as an excuse for further military campaigns. He had long planned to strike southward against the kingdom of the Pondo. In 1828, the year after Nandi died, Shaka announced through an *induna* that since the southern tribes had not wept for Nandi's death, their cattle should be taken from them in the place of tears. The campaign was also to serve as an *ihlambo*, "a washing of the spears" in honor of Nandi.

During this period Shaka seemed consumed by uneasiness. Isaacs wrote, "The restless monarch then took a walk round his premises, as if in deep contemplation, and on his return sent for me; when in conversation, he said, 'I am like a wolf on a flat, that is at a loss for a place to hide his head in'; The Zulus had killed all his principal people and his mother, and he said he would now go to the other side of the water and see King George."

Shaka had become increasingly interested in King George and the English. One of the reasons for the attack to the south was that he wished to open up a direct route of trade between his kingdom and the British settlement at the Cape. A month before he launched his southern campaign, Shaka finally sent his long-delayed embassy to King George, whom he seems to have suspected really lived somewhere in the Cape Colony. Shaka sent many gifts; what he expected in return was good relations with the English and a bottle of Rowland's Macassar Oil.

Shaka tried to induce Fynn and some of the other Port Natal settlers to join his attack on the Pondo with their muskets, but Fynn was extremely wary. He warned Shaka that the Pondo and other southern tribes were looked upon as allies of the English and that an attack on them might be considered the beginning of an attack on the Cape Colony itself. Shaka was aware of the problem and had already warned his *indunas* not to push too far to the south. It was an operation that obviously required great delicacy.

Though Shaka's armies did not in any way encroach upon land claimed by the English, wild rumors began to circulate in the Cape Colony. It was said that the Zulus were planning a mass attack to wipe out the white men. These rumors reached the Cape before Shaka's ambassadors did, and when the ambassadors arrived they were regarded as little better than Zulu spies and given a most unfriendly reception. In exchange for Shaka's magnanimous gifts, the governor of the colony returned only a few meager English goods. Shaka's ambassadors were not even able to obtain a bottle of Rowland's Macassar Oil.

The English sent out a company of troops to block what they feared was a Zulu invasion. The company, under a Major Dundas, encountered a large Bantu force and defeated it badly. Believing he had crushed the Zulu threat, Major Dundas returned to the Cape. In fact, he had not met the Zulus at all but rather the Ngwane led by Matiwane, who had been homeless since their displacement by Zwide many years before.

After being defeated by the British, Matiwane gathered the shattered remnants of his army and tried once again to find a new place to settle. However, another British force, still looking for Zulu attackers (though by this time Shaka had returned to his royal kraal, and his *impis* had been ordered to turn north) encountered Matiwane and his followers and practically wiped them out. Only the old chief himself and a handful of retainers survived the second slaughter. Matiwane then decided to return to his homeland and throw himself upon Shaka's mercy.

The Zulu army had some success in the south, capturing almost all of the Pondo herds. But fear of offending the white colonists by pressing too closely on their border kept the Zulu advance in check, and Shaka did not achieve the sort of overwhelming victory that he had been looking for.

At about this time Shaka's embassy to King George returned from the Cape. Lieutenant King, who had headed the mission, was seriously ill and could not come to see Shaka in person. To Nathaniel Isaacs fell the unhappy task of presenting Shaka with what had been sent in return for his gifts to the English. As Shaka went through the unimpressive collection of English goods, Isaacs slowly became aware that the only thing he was really interested in was Rowland's Macassar Oil. Not finding it, "Shaka was grievously disappointed. Heaving a subdued and bitter sigh he lay down on his mat—and went to sleep."

After this failure, Shaka decided that his choice of ambassadors for the first mission had been a mistake. He promptly began drawing up a list for a second and, he hoped, more reliable expedition.

Despite all the executions he had conducted, Shaka had always been careful to maintain the good will of the bulk of his army, but at this point he made a serious error. The Zulu *impis* marching back from their long southern expedition expected that they would, as usual, be given at least a season's rest. Instead, the twenty thousand troops were ordered to go on marching right past their home kraals and northward to attack Soshangane, who had been gathering a large number of followers and was in the process of setting up a state to rival the Zulu empire. To rouse the sagging spirits of the army, Shaka told them that the northern tribesmen had been taking liberties with Zulu women while the warriors had been away. Shaka, who no longer led all the campaigns in person, remained at his royal kraal, so he was not aware how deep the discontent in his own army was.

When the army marched away, the Zulu king

realized that he had left himself virtually without protection. He therefore dispatched messengers to call back the *udibi* boys—the youngsters who carried the shields, food, and mats for the warriors. They were to be organized into a home guard regiment called "The Bees." As a result the regular warriors were forced to carry their own gear on the long and difficult campaign. After all the sufferings inflicted by Shaka, it was this little extra hardship that sparked an assassination plot against him.

The plot was hatched within the royal family itself. The chief plotters were two of Shaka's half brothers, Dingane (The Needy One) and Mhlangana (The Little Reed). The royal brothers were traveling with the army when the order came that they must carry their own gear. Both decided finally to attempt what they had been contemplating for a long time—to kill Shaka. Dingane and Mhlangana reported that they were sick and had to return home. Shaka was informed of their return but apparently thought nothing of it. He must have regarded both of these half brothers rather lightly, or he never would have allowed them to survive as long as they did.

Also part of the plot was Mbopha, an important *induna* and personal servant of Shaka. Mbopha feared, apparently with justification, that Shaka was planning to get rid of him, because Shaka had told him that in one of his dreams he had a vision that Mbopha was serving a new master.

The moving force behind the plot, however, was Shaka's aunt Mkabayi. Like many old women of Bantu royal families, Mkabayi exercised considerable power. She had been one of Nandi's closest friends. Since Nandi's death, she had turned against the king, becoming convinced that Shaka had poisoned his mother. At least that is the story she spread among her associates. Other enemies of Shaka asserted that Nandi had died as the result of one of the beatings Shaka gave her. There is no evidence to support either of these stories.

Mkabayi had been urging the assassination of Shaka for some time before Dingane and Mhlangana finally decided to act.

The royal brothers reached Shaka's main kraal, Bulawayo, during the third week of September 1828. There they found Mbopha and were informed that Shaka had left for another kraal, Dukuza, farther to the south.

On September 22, the conspirators, short stabbing assegais concealed beneath their cloaks, entered Dukuza, only to discover that Shaka had once again departed. This time he had gone to a small kraal, Nyakamubi (The Bad Year), which was quite nearby. At Nyakamubi they finally caught up with the king. When Dingane, Mhlangana, and Mbopha first saw Shaka he was alone, seated on a stool admiring his cattle, but unexpectedly a group of messengers from the south burst into the kraal. They were bringing gifts of crane feathers and monkey, genet, and otter skins.

The interview with the messengers seemed to go on interminably, and the hour was growing late. Shaka loudly berated the messengers for not having come sooner, when they were expected. The assassins began to fear that if they did not act quickly their plan would miscarry in the darkness. Mbopha rushed into the kraal waving his assegai in one hand and a stick in the other. He struck out at the messengers and cursed them for annoying the king. The bewildered messengers fled. Startled and angry, Shaka rose and demanded to know what Mbopha was doing. As Dingane's stabbing spear struck through his left arm and deep into his back, he screamed and jerked backward. Turning, he saw his brothers glaring at him.

"Children of my father," he shouted, "what is the matter?"

He then summoned his remaining strength and fled through the gate of the kraal, staggered a few paces, and fell. As the assassins stood over him ready to strike the final blows, he pleaded for mercy.

The dying king's final statement is supposed to have been, "Mark my words, you will not rule long. Soon this country will be overrun by white men." Shaka probably didn't say anything of the sort. Prophetic last words are often attributed to great men by writers who already know how events will turn out. But the legend has often been repeated.

Shaka had died alone. Aside from the murderers themselves, only a few cattle guards had witnessed the assassination, and they had run away at once.

The assassins' plans went no farther than the killing itself. They had not even decided what to do with the king's body. It was getting very dark, and the thought of being confronted with Shaka's ghost in the night was terrifying. The conspirators left the body where it fell, assuming that hyenas would take care of the problem during the night.

When the three men returned to Nyakamubi in the morning they found that Shaka's body had not been touched by scavengers, although fresh footprints showed that hyenas had circled it. The murderers assumed that the king's supernatural powers had protected his corpse, and they decided to give Shaka a proper, if hasty, burial.

While preparations for the burial were going on, a crowd began to assemble, for news of the assassination had been spread by the cattle guards. Those who came to watch were too stunned to do anything.

One of Shaka's loyal vassals, Chief Sotobe, and a few of his followers arrived unexpectedly. Chief Sotobe denounced the murderers and called upon those who were watching the burial to rise up and kill the regicides. But Dingane and Mhlangana reminded the crowd of all the hardships they had suffered during Shaka's reign. They described the time of Shaka's father, Senzangakona, as a lost golden age that would return now that the tyrant was dead. The people just stood there. Finally, Chief Sotobe confessed that he, too, had lately been distressed by Shaka's excesses. And so the burial continued.

When the ceremony was nearly complete, Nomxamana, one of Shaka's praise singers, rushed into the kraal and flung himself onto the corpse of his master. He called out hysterically for the spirits to destroy the murderers and begged that he too be allowed to die in the way that Shaka had. Dingane and Mhlangana quickly obliged him.

The murderers wrapped Shaka's huge body in the skin of an ox that had been slaughtered for the occasion and tumbled it into an unused grain pit. The makeshift grave was unmarked, and its exact location has long since been forgotten. Today the remains of one of the greatest and most terrible warriors the world has ever seen rest somewhere on Cupper Street in the village of Stanger, South Africa.

X

What Manner of Man?

SHAKA'S STORY does not really end with his inglorious death. He had held power for a little over ten years. His appearance as a political and military force has been called "abrupt, brief, and bloody." Yet after Shaka, nothing could ever be the same again.

Shaka's accomplishments were enormous. A. T. Bryant, an Englishman who lived in South Africa during the final years of the nineteenth century and who wrote extensively about the Zulus, tried to explain what Shaka had been able to do in terms that his fellow Englishmen might understand:

"Had the British Army in 1879 found Zululand occupied not by a single united nation requiring only a single concentration of attention, but by a hundred independent kingdoms, each demanding separate treatment; and had that British Army consisted of but a single battalion of a few hundred strong which was all Shaka could at first muster; and had it been equipped with a single assegai per man and lacked all commissariat, we should have been able to understand more clearly the vastness and complexity of the task undertaken single-handed and accomplished without hitch or hindrance by the mighty Shaka in his conquest, not only of Zululand, but of the whole region between Delagoa Bay and Matata. We are no longer surprised at his untiring activity. To achieve such a tremendous result, and that within the space of a short reign . . . uninterrupted warfare was of absolute necessity."

Looking at the scope of Shaka's conquests, it becomes impossible to deny that he possessed military and political genius of a very high order. Most of those who have written about him give lip service to his genius, but go on to denounce him as a savage, a monster, and a madman. Those few who are sympathetic often try to deny that he did many of the terrible things that he most assuredly did do.

Shaka is not the sort of figure who can be approached with cool objectivity. He stirs strong emotions in everyone who has studied his history. The problem of evaluating his motives is immeasurably complicated by the fact that he was black, while most of those who have written about him, including the present writer, are white.

Shaka lived in what is now the Republic of South Africa, a country in which a small minority of whites still rule a large majority of blacks, among them the descendants of Shaka's Zulus. It is con-

venient for the whites of South Africa to think of
Shaka as a savage and a monster and uncomfortable
for them to admit that the blacks, whom they consider inferior, have possessed leaders of genius. But
Shaka is far from a universal hero among black
Africans. Many of the peoples who suffered directly
or indirectly from Zulu conquests tend to regard
Shaka as a force for evil. Should Shaka then be
considered a hero of the oppressed, or one of the
oppressors? The question is unanswerable.

The single overwhelming fact that must be confronted in attempting to evaluate Shaka is his continual use of terror, both to carve out his empire and
to maintain it. The terror was of two basic types:
military terror, used against external enemies; and
civil terror, used against those who were already part
of his state.

Shaka's military terror is easier to understand,
simply because we have witnessed so much of the
same sort of thing throughout history. *Impi ebomvu,*
under one name or another, has been employed by
conquerors of all eras and from all parts of the
world. In Biblical times the Assyrians boasted of wiping out the populations of entire cities and razing the
cities to the ground. The Crusaders massacred
Moslems and Christians alike, regardless of sex and
age. The list of horrors could be extended almost
indefinitely, for in modern times technology has made
total warfare, warfare conducted against civilian populations as well as soldiers, almost a necessity.

Is there any effective difference between a group
of warriors who enter a village, stab the inhabitants,

and burn their huts to the ground, and a group of fliers who destroy a village with bombs and napalm, burning huts and villagers alike? For the fliers, the killing is more impersonal; they never see their victims. But this is hardly likely to be of any comfort to the victims.

Both these methods of destruction are forms of military terrorism, and both can be very effective. Are the men who order the bombings of the villages savages and monsters, or simply good soldiers doing their job? One cannot logically condemn Shaka on the one hand and yet excuse modern generals for doing the same thing.

Shaka was a more ambitious conqueror than the other Bantu kings of his day, or if not more ambitious (for who knows what dreams of empire lay in the mind of someone like Zwide?), at least more successful. But this does not necessarily make him a monster either, unless one considers all successful conquerors monsters. Shaka was no more ambitious than Alexander the Great, Julius Caesar, or Napoleon, yet these three European conquerors are widely admired as heroes. We must judge Shaka by the same set of standards. As a military strategist he may well have been the equal of any of them.

Shaka's civil terror, the terror directed against his own subjects, and even against his own officials, is not so easy to understand. It was the continual round of brutal executions observed and recorded by Fynn and Isaacs that was primarily responsible for giving Shaka the reputation of a madman and a monster. The number and apparent casualness of the killings, rather than the huge armies, the superb discipline, or the vast herds of cattle, are what most impressed the white observers at Shaka's court. Fynn and Isaacs described the executions repeatedly with a sort of horrified fascination. Here is a typical scene, as described by Fynn:

"Cattle and war formed the whole subject of his [Shaka's] conversations: and during his sitting, while in the act of taking a pinch of snuff, or when engaged in the deepest conversation, he would by a movement of his finger, perceivable only by his attendants, point out one of the gathering sitting around him, upon which, to the surprise of strangers, the man would be carried off and killed. This was a daily occurrence. On one occasion I witnessed 60 boys under 12 years of age dispatched before he had breakfasted. No sooner is the signal given, and the object pointed out, than those sitting around him scramble to kill him, although they have good reason to expect the next moment the same fate themselves, but such apprehensions are far from their thoughts; the will of the King being uppermost.

"I have seen instances where they have had the opportunities of speaking while being carried off, but which they always employed in enthusiastically praising the heroic deeds of their King."

Although most of the condemned persons did not resist execution, and some actually seemed to assist in their own deaths, not all the condemned were so cooperative. Perhaps it was an indication of a growing mood of rebelliousness that just a week before Shaka's assassination, Isaacs witnessed this scene:

Shaka was seated, "with about two hundred people forming a half circle, with a few chiefs sitting near him, trying six prisoners for stealing corn. We had scarcely been seated a few moments when the despot ordered the prisoners for immediate execution. Two of them, stout, able fellows, tried to make their escape by leaping over us with great agility, and making good use of their speed; but the warriors finally secured them, and stoned them to death."

Shaka's childhood was an extremely unhappy one, and perhaps this affected his personality. Many have theorized that his early rejection caused him to become a sadist, who enjoyed inflicting pain upon others. But neither Fynn nor Isaacs, who were on the scene, believed that Shaka enjoyed the killings he ordered or that he was mad. On the contrary, they suspected that the apparently casual and purposeless executions were part of a well-planned show of power, like the exhibitions of cattle and dancing. Isaacs commented after witnessing one series of executions that they had been done "merely to terrify us." This they did, for the Europeans came to fear Shaka, though he had never made any threatening moves toward them.

Shaka may have been driven by thoughts and desires that we would today consider abnormal or even insane, but as far as we know, he did not ever reveal his inner hopes, desires, or fears to anyone. Occasionally he appeared to go into a frenzy of emotion, as after Nandi's death. Yet there is sufficient evidence to allow us to conclude that even these displays were more a matter of policy than of genuine emotion, or madness.

Certainly it is not necessary to believe that Shaka was mad in order to explain his actions. Casual executions were common features of the courts in many lands.

Timur (Tamerlane), the fourteenth-century Moslem conqueror, used to hold great banquets for his important officials or emirs, a regular feature of which was that executioners would enter the hall, drag out one or more of the emirs, and kill them for crimes, real or imaginary, against the ruler. It was Timur's desire to keep his officials dangling "betwixt hope and fear." Shaka could easily have adopted the same motto.

A nineteenth-century Burmese king was more refined in the matter of casual executions, but the results were the same, as this eyewitness account indicates:

"Sudden deaths were not at all uncommon in the late king's reign. An official displeased him in some way and Mindohn Min said emphatically, 'I don't want to see that man any more.' The poor wretch left the royal presence to be seized by lictors outside and killed more or less rapidly. A day or two afterwards his majesty would ask where so-and-so was. 'Alas! sire,' was the answer, 'he died of chagrin shortly after the lord of the earth and ocean cast eyes of displeasure on him. . . .' [the king] made a special boast that never in all his reign had he ordered an execution. Yet many people died of 'official colic' during the time he was on the throne. . . ."

Shaka's biographer, E. A. Ritter, who interviewed many Zulus, including a few who had been alive in Shaka's time, came to the conclusion that Shaka used terror to hold his state together because he believed that nothing else would work. Ritter has Shaka say:

"Terror is the only thing they [the Zulus] understand, and you can rule Zulus only by killing them. Who are the Zulus? They are parts of two hundred or more unruly clans which I had to break up and reshape, and only the fear of death will hold them together."

And again:

"I need no bodyguard at all, for even the bravest men who approach me get weak at the knees and their hearts turn to water, whilst their heads become giddy and incapable of thinking as the sweat of fear paralyzes them. They know no other will except that of their King, who is something above, and below, this earth."

The statements are imaginary, but they make sense. Shaka might well have said or thought such things. On the other hand, he may never have formulated a coherent policy of terror but simply have taken care of problems in the best way he knew how, by killing them off.

Shaka's successors, as well as several other Bantu kings of the time, adopted systems in which violence was used almost as often as Shaka used it. Nor are terroristic systems particular to African or Oriental peoples or to people who live in relatively simple societies. Ivan IV of Russia, called The Terrible, used methods surprisingly similar to those employed by Shaka to raise the power of the czar and crush the powerful and independent nobles. For all his terror, and at least partly because of it, Ivan was considered a great man, one of the founders of the Russian state.

In modern times, the Russian people supported Stalin's terror, the German people Hitler's terror. In both nations, many lived in perpetual fear of "the knock at the door"—arrest by the secret police or the Gestapo—the modern equivalent of a nod of Shaka's head.

Eugene Victor Walter, an American scholar, made a study of terroristic despotisms—tribes or states in which a single powerful ruler maintains himself by constantly killing or threatening to kill his subjects. A major portion of this study was devoted to Shaka's Zulu empire. Walter's book includes what he calls an "ideal despotic 'constitution,'" of which the preamble is fashioned to read like the preamble of the United States Constitution:

"We the people of the Despot, including the greater and lesser officials chosen by him and formerly sovereign chiefs who have submitted to his will, rejoicing in the terrible majesty and radiant grandeur of the Master who has thrown his shield over us, in order to form a more perfect union, to conquer all peoples who do not submit, and to gather the wealth of the land which is his by right and by power, do pledge our lives, our honor, our children, and our efforts to magnify his glory, to immolate our wills in his service, to render ourselves, all people and all things to dust at his command."

Though it appears that the despot rules entirely by his own will, and in fact he actively seeks to make people believe he does, he must have the support of his people, and of those officials chosen to carry out his commands. In the end, Shaka overreached himself. From the time of Nandi's death, he seems to have lost touch with his people and even with his *indunas*. They were asked to bear more than they could. For several months before his death, Shaka's assassination was being freely predicted throughout Zululand.

Dingane and Mhlangana had probably hated Shaka from the moment he took the Zulu throne. Both were of royal blood; both had some claim to the throne themselves. They could hardly have regarded Shaka as anything but a usurper. Yet they remained subservient for years while Shaka's power grew. Only when they felt that Shaka had lost the support of the Zulu people did they dare to act.

Shaka was dead, but the nation he had forged from the "parts of two hundred or more unruly clans" remained. And as its people were soon to discover, so did the terror.

XI

Wrong Time, Wrong Place

EITHER OF THE TWO ROYAL BROTHERS who had been Shaka's assassins might have claimed the Zulu throne. There could be no such institution as a dual kingship. One of the brothers would rule; the other would almost certainly have to die. The irony was that the new king could never trust a killer of kings, even when, he, too, had participated in the act.

Dingane and Mhlangana agreed to wait until the bulk of the Zulu army returned from fighting Soshangane in the north before any decision was made. Of the two, Dingane, being the older, had a far stronger claim to the throne, though he may not have been the more intelligent or the more able.

Both brothers tried to gain the support of the third

of Shaka's assassins, Mbopha. Mhlangana reportedly
told Mbopha that Dingane was unfit to rule and
that he should be assassinated. Mbopha said he had
been thinking along the same lines but reported the
conversation to Dingane, with whom he had already
thrown in his lot. Even more significantly, Dingane
had gained the support of old Mkabayi, the most
powerful of the Zulu women and the real driving
force behind Shaka's assassination.

No one knew exactly where the army was, when
it would return, or what the reaction of the *indunas*
and men would be to the news of Shaka's death. The
brothers waited and watched one another carefully
and with increasing distrust. Then one night early in
November, an unknown assailant threw a spear at
Dingane and wounded him, though not seriously.
Dingane immediately went into hiding. Both sides
mustered their supporters, and it seemed that there
might be civil war. Mkabayi summoned Mhlangana
and told him that she had arranged a meeting between
him and Dingane at which they could try to patch
up their differences. Since neither brother trusted the
other, she said, both must come alone and unarmed.
Mhlangana did so, but Dingane failed to appear. Instead, he sent four of his henchmen, who dragged
Mhlangana off and murdered him.

Dingane had himself proclaimed king of the Zulus.
All those who presented an immediate danger to his
regime were killed. Then Dingane settled down to
wait for the return of the Zulu army. It was the
leading *indunas* who would decide whether Dingane's
kingship would survive.

While this was going on, the campaign against Soshangane in the north had turned into a disaster. From the very first, the attack had been a mistake. The army had been asked to fight in the sweltering and unhealthy subtropical region (by going north they had moved closer to the equator) in the spring, rather than waiting until the following winter. The army was tired, for they had recently fought a long campaign in the south, the land was unfamiliar, and the campaign had been so hastily planned that the Zulus were not even sure where they were going. They marched well past Soshangane's stronghold before they discovered their mistake and turned back.

Soshangane knew that his meager forces could not hope to stand against the Zulus, but he had learned lessons in tactics and strategy from Shaka during the Second Ndwandwe War, when a great Ndwandwe force under Soshangane's command was defeated. At that time it was the Ndwandwes who had the larger army, so Shaka had avoided open battle until the Ndwandwes were tired, hungry, and discouraged. Now Soshangane turned the same tactics against the Zulus. He even sent his warriors into the Zulu camp at night to stab sleeping soldiers, just as the Zulus had done against him. Soshangane never gained a victory in battle, but the Zulus were so worn down by their long campaign and by Soshangane's harassing tactics that their army reached the point of collapse.

Facing disaster in the field, the Zulu *indunas* decided to turn around and go home. They had suffered heavy casualties and had failed to capture so much as a single head of Soshangane's cattle. Every man in the returning army was tortured by visions of Shaka's wrath and of the mass executions that would surely follow. Some of the *indunas* deserted; others committed suicide. But the mass of the army marched fatalistically back toward Zululand, unaware that Shaka was dead.

Somewhere between the Mkuze and Black Umfolozi rivers, messengers met the troops and told them of Shaka's assassination and of the occupation of the throne by Dingane. A wave of hysterical rejoicing broke out. Men who believed that their lives had been forfeit felt as though they had received a last-minute pardon. When the army marched into Zululand they hailed Dingane as a liberator.

Dingane played his part by appearing humble and grateful. He assured the army that there would be no mass executions for the failure of the campaign in the north, which had been Shaka's fault anyway. Everything, he said, would now be different. The great traditions of the past, which Shaka had so ruthlessly trampled, would be restored and respected. The women would be released from the royal harems and allowed to become the wives of the *indunas* and elders. All Zulu men who had reached full maturity would be free to put on the headring and to marry, raise children, tend their cattle, and enjoy the fruits of peace. The time of perpetual warfare was over. Even the hereditary chiefs of the conquered clans would be restored to their rightful positions, provided, of course, that they remained loyal to the Zulu king. The Zulus, who had faced so many hardships, were almost overcome with joy. It seemed like the dawning of a golden age.

The Europeans at Port Natal were stunned by the news of Shaka's death. They did not know what to make of his successor, Dingane, because none of them had ever met him. He had been so obscure during Shaka's lifetime that few had even heard his name. But Dingane soon won them over. Isaacs wrote that the Zulu, "have now a ruler who has begun to govern with judgement and to exercise his power with discretion." Isaacs noted that Dingane intended to turn spears into dancing sticks, the Zulu equivalent of beating swords into plowshares.

He also wrote, "Dingane certainly is destined to please his people, for he has the ways of a savage courtier, and seeks every moment to show that he wishes rather to reign in the good opinion of his subjects than to rule over them with the arm of terror."

Fynn claimed that he had distrusted the new king from the start, but that claim was made many years after he first met Dingane, and the desire to appear a prophet may well have caused him to alter his original impressions.

Not everyone was enthusiastic about Dingane, however. Nqetho, chief of the large Qwabe tribe, was one of the few local chiefs who had been allowed to retain a considerable degree of autonomy under Shaka. The original chief of the Qwabe, Pakatwayo, had been killed by Shaka, and Nqetho, his brother, placed on the throne. Nqetho had remained a devoted supporter of Shaka and had received many favors from him. Under a new ruler Nqetho feared he might lose his favored status. A small point of dispute arose between Dingane and Nqetho. Dingane could have ignored the incident or given in on it, but instead he demanded complete subordination. Nqetho feared that this would be the new order of things, and he led the Qwabe into open revolt.

Dingane promptly sent the Zulu army to crush the rebels, but when the two armies met, nothing happened. The Zulus and the Qwabe had often fought on the same side in Shaka's wars, and were apparently unwilling to kill one another. Both forces simply retired from the field without a battle. The Zulus' unwillingness to fight had undoubtedly been encouraged by Dingane's announcement that the practice of executing "cowards" and liquidating defeated regiments would be abandoned.

Still, Nqetho feared that Dingane would try to revenge himself and decided to abandon his homeland. The Qwabe thus became another in the stream of refugees fleeing from the Zulus and cutting their own bloody roads through all the lands they passed.

The Qwabe revolt had been unexpectedly successful, and the behavior of the usually disciplined Zulu *impis* had been a shock. The new Zulu king now faced a crisis. He knew he would either have to try to establish the Zulu empire on an entirely different basis, which would probably involve much less power for the ruler and a much smaller territory under his control, or he would have to reassert control as Shaka had done, by terror. Dingane chose the path of terror.

The daily round of executions in the Zulu court

began once again. All chiefs suspected of disloyalty were put to death, despite Dingane's pledge to restore their rights. The Zulu king was no longer able to tolerate his coconspirator, Mbopha. Mbopha had helped to kill one king; perhaps he would help to kill another. Besides, his very presence reminded people that disloyalty to a reigning monarch might bring high rewards. Mbopha was executed, and men like Chief Sotobe, who had faithfully spoken out in favor of Shaka (and, incidentally, against Dingane himself) were restored to favor. What Dingane needed most was men who had shown a devotion to royalty.

Dingane also reasserted control over the rights of his warriors to marry, although he exercised this control more liberally than Shaka ever had. Dingane released many of Shaka's "sisters" from the seraglios, but retained some three hundred of them for himself. Like Shaka, he made it a policy never to marry and beget an heir who might become a threat to him.

As his royal residence Dingane constructed a huge kraal that he called Emgungundlovu—"The Place Surrounded by Elephants." It was a name calculated to inspire fear.

At about this time Chief Matiwane of the wandering Ngwane returned to Zululand, hoping to seek Shaka's mercy. Instead he found Dingane on the throne, and Dingane showed no mercy at all. Dingane feared that the famous old warrior would become the nucleus for rebellion. He ordered Matiwane taken to the place of execution, a ridge outside the royal kraal. There the executioners gouged out the old chief's eyes, hammered wooden pegs up his nostrils, and beat him to death. The horror aroused by this execution led people to call the executioner's ridge "Matiwane's hill," and it became notorious throughout southern Africa.

Although Dingane used many of Shaka's terroristic methods, he did not possess Shaka's military genius. The Zulu *impis,* which had been accustomed to victory, were now forced to face defeat, often humiliating defeat. The fault was not entirely Dingane's—times had changed and the surrounding tribes had begun to adopt the military techniques developed by Shaka, using them with increasing effectiveness against the Zulus themselves.

But the real threat to Dingane and the Zulus came from the white men who were streaming into Zulu territory in alarmingly large numbers. Dingane attempted to maintain the good relations that Shaka had established with the English at Port Natal, but the problems were more complicated now, and the strains more frequent. The whites were demanding more concessions and had the power to back their demands.

Jakot, "The Swimmer," continually warned Dingane that the white men were planning to take over all of Zululand, and the legend of Shaka's last words about the white men was repeated frequently. Dingane wavered. Often he granted extravagant favors to the Port Natal settlers. When he refused a request he blamed his *indunas,* proclaiming that he personally had nothing but the friendliest of intentions.

Jakot had become a real problem to the whites, and Fynn finally persuaded Dingane that the man was a liar and that he was hurting relations between the Zulus and Port Natal. The Zulu king ordered the interpreter's execution, but he demanded that the white men kill him—which, after some hesitation, they did in February 1832.

A more immediate threat to the Zulus came from the Boers. The Boers hated the English, who had made themselves the masters of the Cape. Many Boers sought to escape English control by migrating into the interior, beginning what has been called The Great Trek. The destination of the trekboers was Natal, which they believed they could take from the Zulus by trickery or force.

Dingane disliked and distrusted the Boers, but he respected their guns and horses. When a group of Boers led by Piet Retief visited him to ask for land, he greeted them with apparent warmth. Dingane requested that the Boers help the Zulus recapture some stolen cattle, which they did. Afterward Dingane invited Retief and his men to a celebration at Emgungundlovu on February 3, 1838. While the dancing went on, Dingane cried out, "Kill the wizards!" All the Boers were dragged to "Matiwane's hill" and executed.

Dingane had hoped to destroy the Boer threat completely by wiping out the trekkers while retaining the friendship of the English, but he had miscalculated badly. The Zulus were placed under increasing pressure from white invaders and Dingane was eventually forced to sign a treaty in which he was required to abandon to the Boers not only all of Natal, but also a portion of the Zulu heartland, north of the Tugela River.

This humiliation placed intolerable strains on the proud Zulus. Many refused to follow Dingane and sought protection among the whites. Among those who did so was Dingane's younger brother, Mpande (The Root). Mpande had a claim to the Zulu throne, and Dingane had once been determined to have him killed. He was persuaded not to because so much royal Zulu blood had already been spilled. Furthermore, Mpande was considered too simple-minded and easy-going to be any threat.

Mpande accepted the protection of the Boers, who saw in him a conveniently pliable successor to the troublesome Dingane. As Dingane's star waned, the number of Mpande's followers increased dramatically. Ultimately, armed with the promise of Boer support, Mpande was able to challenge Dingane. The decisive battle was fought at Magongo in February 1840, and Mpande's forces prevailed. The Boers never had to fire a shot. Dingane fled but could find no friendly refuge. He was put to death by a minor chief he had offended some years before.

Mpande had gained the throne with Boer support; he paid for it with huge numbers of Zulu cattle, and by becoming virtually a vassal of the whites. His reign was long and uneventful, but he maintained good relations with both the Boers and the British. During this period of peace, the vigor of the Zulu nation, which had been sapped during Dingane's turbulent years, was restored.

Mpande died in 1873. For some years before that he had become too feeble to be anything more than a figurehead. Effective rule of the Zulus had passed into the hands of one of his sons, Cetshwayo, in whom the Zulus found another great leader. Unfortunately, he had arrived too late.

By this time the British had determined to crush Zulu power entirely and issued an ultimatum that demanded the virtual destruction of the Zulu kingdom. Cetshwayo had no illusions concerning the relative fighting effectiveness of guns and assegais and did everything in his power to avoid a war. But the British were intransigent, and the Zulu warriors, raised on the martial traditions of Shaka, demanded that a stand be made. British forces advanced into Zululand in January 1879. At Isandhlwana they met the Zulus and were wiped out. It was the most stunning defeat that any modern army has ever suffered at the hands of "savages."

However, Zulu glory was short-lived. In 1879 Victorian England was the mightiest military nation in the world. Overwhelming British strength was mobilized, and though Cetshwayo continued to seek an honorable peace, the British attacked his capital, Ulundi. In this final battle the Zulu warriors marched with perfect discipline in their "head, horns, and chest formation" into the barrels of the British guns. But courage and discipline meant little in the face of superior weapons. The Zulus were defeated, and Cetshwayo was taken prisoner.

The British tried to break up the Zulu nation into the separate tribes out of which it had been formed, but the experiment didn't work. Finally, in 1883, they were forced to bring Cetshwayo back to restore order. But it was too late even for that. An old internal dispute flared up once again, and the Zulus were split into two warring factions. Cetshwayo's followers were slaughtered, and the king himself was forced into hiding. He died the following year, possibly of poison.

As a political unit the Zulu nation no longer existed. However, it was not forgotten. In a recent series of books on African history prepared by Ibadan University in Nigeria, Professor John D. Omer-Cooper has written:

"Under white rule, traditions of the exploits of earlier days have been kept alive in songs and stories and to this day the old men become enthusiastic when they talk about the kings and they love to recite their praises. The fame of the Zulu name and the fact that Europeans tend to use it indiscriminately for all the Nguni-speaking Bantu of Natal has led to a situation where many, who were never part of Shaka's state, now believe and feel themselves to belong to the Zulu people. The work of Shaka in creating a sense of unity wider than the traditional is still continuing."

ZULU SPELLING AND PRONUNCIATION

THE TRANSLITERATION of the Zulu language into English is at best uncertain. The main problem is that Zulu contains several sounds not used in English. There are, for example, three distinct tongue clicks in Zulu speech.

The Zulus also use prefixes unknown in English. For example, Shaka's mother's clan is referred to in this book as the Langeni, though the name might more properly be spelled emaLangeni or even Emalangeni. Most personal names also have a prefix. Thus Shaka is really uShaka; and Zulu, strictly speaking, is amaZulu. I have tried to use spellings that will be most familiar and least confusing to the average reader.

The following pronunciations (from Donald R. Morris's *The Washing of the Spears*) might be helpful as examples.

Shaka	Oo-*sha*-ge	Mpande	Mm-*pan*-de
Dingiswayo	Di-ngis-*why*-o	Cetshwayo	Tsk-tsh-*why*-o
Dingane	Di-*nga*-nyeh		

A GLOSSARY OF ZULU AND
SOUTH AFRICAN TERMS

ASSEGAI — A spear for throwing or stabbing.

BOERS — Descendants of Dutch settlers in South Africa. Also called Afrikaners.

BULAWAYO — Shaka's royal kraal—"The Place of Killing."

DUBI — Boys who carried supplies for the warriors.

EMGUNGUNDLOVU — Dingane's royal kraal—"The Place Surrounded by Elephants."

IHLAMBO — A ceremonial "washing of the spears" in the blood of enemies—roughly, revenge.

IMBONGI — Official praise singers of the king.

IMPI — A regiment of warriors.

IMPI EBOMVU — "Red Impi"—total warfare.

INDUNAS — The headmen.

ISANGOMA — Witch finders or magicians.

IXWA — Shaka's short stabbing assegai.

KNOBKERRIES — Clubs with knobs on the end used in warfare.

KRAAL — Enclosure, usually a Bantu village or circular grouping of huts.

LOBOLA — A dowry of cattle.

MFECANE — "The Crushing" or the chain of migrations associated with the expansion of the Zulu empire.

NGUNI — A related group of Bantu dialects and a collective name for the people who speak them.

NTAGNA — A military grouping in Dingiswayo's army.

SIGIDI — A large number, a thousand.

TREKBOERS — Those Boers who took part in The Great Trek from the southern tip of Africa to Zulu territory.

UMTAKATI — Evildoers or wizards.

SUGGESTED FOR FURTHER READING

BECKER, PETER *Dingane, King of the Zulu*. New York: Thomas Y. Crowell, 1965. A thorough biography of Shaka's half brother, murderer, and successor.

——— *Path of Blood*. London: Longmans, Green, 1962. A study of the career of Mzilikazi, who was, next to Shaka, the most interesting of the Nguni conquerors.

BRYANT, A. T. *Olden Times in Zululand and Natal*. London: Longmans, Green, 1929. A massive collection of tribal lore based on interviews with Zulu elders and others during the late nineteenth and early twentieth centuries.

——— *The Zulu People*. Pietermaritzburg, South Africa: Shuter and Shooter, 1949. A detailed study of the Zulus by a missionary who lived among them.

FYNN, HENRY FRANCIS *The Diary of Henry Francis Fynn,* edited by J. Stuart and D. Mck Malcom. Pietermaritzburg, South Africa: Shuter and Shooter, 1950. Although not exactly a diary, since it was written years after the events it describes, Fynn's book provides an unparalleled look at the Zulu kingdom as it was under Shaka.

ISAACS, NATHANIEL *Travels and Adventures in Eastern Africa* (two volumes). London: Edward Churton, 1836. Along with Fynn's "diary," a basic source for the life and times of Shaka.

JULY, ROBERT W. *A History of the African People*. New York: Charles Scribner's Sons, 1970. A new and thorough history of black Africa, from ancient times to the present day.

KRIGE, EILEEN *The Social System of the Zulu*. London: Longmans, Green, 1936. An excellent account of the daily life of the Zulus, written by a trained anthropologist.

MORRIS, DONALD R. *The Washing of the Spears*. New York: Simon & Schuster, 1965. A dramatically written history that concentrates on the Zulu War of 1879 but provides information on Shaka's time and before. The author tends to the view that Shaka was simply a monster.

OMER-COOPER, JOHN D. *The Zulu Aftermath.* Evanston, Ill.: Northwestern University Press, 1966. An excellent scholarly account of the rise of the Zulu empire and of what happened to the people scattered by the *Mfecane.*

RITTER, E. A. *Shaka Zulu.* London: Longmans, Green, 1955. A sympathetic and very readable biography of Shaka. The book is, however, highly fictionalized.

WALTER, E. V. *Terror and Resistance.* New York: Oxford University Press, 1969. A political study of terroristic states, with major emphasis on Shaka's empire. This is a unique treatment of Shaka as a political figure rather than as an anthropological curiosity.

FOR YOUNGER READERS

STEED, JENNY *The Voice of the Great Elephant.* New York: Pantheon, 1968. A novel about a young Zulu boy growing up during Shaka's time.

VLAHOS, OLIVIA *African Beginnings.* New York: Viking Press, 1967. A survey of African history and anthropology.

Articles

GLUCKMAN, MAX *The Rise of the Zulu Empire. Scientific American,* April 1960. A good, brief analysis of Shaka's state.

INDEX

About the Author

Born in Chicago, Daniel Cohen graduated from the journalism school of the University of Illinois and then became an editor for *Science Digest*, where he worked for ten years. Since becoming a free-lance writer he has published some twenty books for young people and adults. His most recent books include *Watchers in the Wild*, *Talking with the Animals*, *A Natural History of Unnatural Things*, and *In Search of Ghosts*. His articles have appeared in such magazines as *The Nation*, *Coronet*, and *Pageant*. Mr. Cohen and his wife and four-year-old daughter live near Monticello, New York.

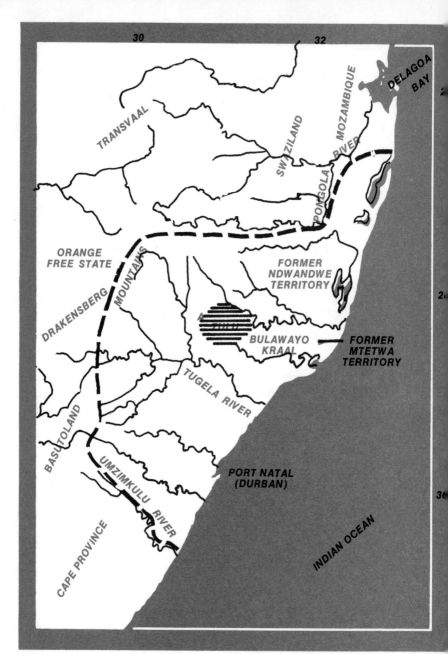

(a) The land originally occupied by the Zulus before Shaka's time.   Shaka'
empire at its height (long broken line).The territory controlled by the Zul
covered 80,000 square miles.